Witness to Love

Witness to Love

How to Help the Next Generation
Build Marriages That Survive and Thrive

Ryan & Mary-Rose Verret

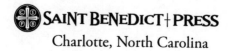

SAINT BENEDICT + PRESS
Charlotte, North Carolina

Cataloging-in-Publication data on file with the Library of Congress.

ISBN: 978-1-61890-065-4

Cover design by Caroline Kiser

Published in the United States by
Saint Benedict Press, LLC
PO Box 410487
Charlotte, NC 28241
www.SaintBenedictPress.com

Printed and bound in the United States of America.

This book is lovingly dedicated to all those dear friends who have shared their witness and marriages with us. We will also treasure and hold dear the stories of your lives that produced so many moments of laughter and redeeming tears!

To Saint Pope John Paul II, thank you for your love, wisdom, and pastoral guidance during the most formative years of our lives! Even beyond your passing, you continue to remind us that we are loved unconditionally by our Father. We love you!

To Saint Joseph, you have always been a dear friend of our family. Thank you.

To Saints Louis & Zelie Martin, we thank you for the sacrificial witness to love that you lived out every day of your married lives. You are an enduring model of the marital charity!

To all the priests and religious whom we call friends. We have learned so much from you as through your generosity, joy, and commitment to Christ and His Church. Your own personal witness to love is an essential nuptial sign in the world directing us all to the ultimate wedding feast of the Lamb!

Table of Contents

Foreword ix

Introduction: If Love is Not
Revealed to Them 1

1 A State of Dis-Union:
The Divorce Effect 7

2 Do You Have What it Takes? 21

3 Who Has Time for Mentoring?! 33

4 The Mentorless Generation's Need
for Solidarity 39

5 Saying "I Do" Each Day:
The Heart of Our Marriage 59

6 Inside A Mentor Couple's Heart:
The Agony & the Ecstasy
of Marriage 71

7 Mentoring the "Unmarried" 85

8 After "I Do": Continuing
the Mentorship 111

9 True Tales of Happily Ever After . . 129

10   The Shared Fruits of the
      Mentor Model. 139
11   A Special Vocation:
      Saving Troubled Marriages 147
12   Marriage: A Glimpse of Heaven . . . 159

A Note to Clergy 169
Notes 171
Bibliography. 181
Resources 187
Acknowledgements 191
About the Authors 195

Foreword

WALT Disney once said: "It's kind of fun to do the impossible!" Imagine if we could convince you that you had an essential role in fighting the divorce statistics. Imagine if you could help reverse the divorce statistics by preparing young couples for marriages that will stand the test of time. We know this may sound as "long ago" and "far, far away" as the those fairy tales filled with beautiful impossibilities and romantic dreams that our five-year old daughter loves to hear. Who today really believes that we can live happily ever after, especially with a member of the opposite sex? We do!

This book will help you prepare young engaged couples for marriage by providing them with a firm foundation to begin their marriage and offering enduring support as they walk forward those crucial first years. Despite our over-connected world, young couples are increasingly unaware of how to discern commitment and how to strengthen and protect their future marriages.

How do you encourage cohabiting couples to discern marriage? How can you help to break the cycle of divorce? You can do this simply by sharing the good in your marriage with young couples. Let them learn from your mistakes, struggles, discoveries, and triumphs. Share with them your real life, and show them the love you have for one another.

You may be thinking: "Our marriage isn't perfect. How can we do this?" Well, our marriage isn't perfect, and that *is* the point.

It is through sharing imperfections that our love grows, and our appreciation for God's original plan for marriage deepens. If we wait until we are perfect to share our lives, we will miss out and so will those young couples whom God has put in our lives! This book is dedicated to those couples who have touched our marriage with insights from their own. Our hearts are full of awe and appreciation for them.

It is with gratitude for their candor, humility, determination, and self-sacrifice that we, too, would like to share stories of those who are true witnesses to love. We hope to inspire you to share your marriage, imperfect though it may be, with those who do not understand how to live out the sacrament of marriage. If God found you worthy enough to be married, then you *are* qualified to be a witness! A lamp is not meant to be put under a bushel basket, so let your marriage shine before all so that they can see the good works that God is doing in our world today (see Matthew 5:15)!

Married couples who share their witness are on the front lines battling *the* critical problem in the world today— splintered and broken families. We do not need perfect couples to change the world. Rather, the world needs married couples who are committed to each other, to their families, and to God. Through your example, young couples will learn about God, His love for them, and His desire for their future.

In our experience couples are not attracted to the appearance of perfection but are drawn to making their marriage more stable in an ever-changing world. A stable marriage is one that has the luster of a sacrament, the uplifting example of self-sacrifice, the joy of mutual dedication, and the ability to forgive. Perfection is not required to be a witness to the love of God and to the beauty of His sacraments. Simply strive to live and to love in conformity with God's desire for your marriage, and you will change the world.

Introduction

Man cannot live without love. He remains a being that is incomprehensible for himself, his life is senseless, if love is not revealed to him, if he does not encounter love, if he does not experience it and make it his own, if he does not participate intimately in it.[1]

Saint John Paul II in *Redemptor Hominis*

I cannot remember why I (Mary-Rose) first asked this question of an engaged couple back in 2008. I do not remember the couple's name or even what they looked like, but I do remember their response which shocked me and is the reason for this book.

Each week I would have a one-time meeting with an engaged couple to discuss their "Pre-Marital Inventory" (the results of a long list of questions that couples often need to answer and discuss prior to their wedding). It was often a challenging meeting and to keep things moving I would use a few "ice-breaker" questions if a couple was simply giving yes or no answers.

One day, when meeting with a newly engaged couple, I was struck by their unhealthy isolation from friends and family. They lived in their own world, preventing them from welcoming input from others. In their isolated world, there were no markers against which they could measure the impossible height of their expectations of marriage. The insights of close, loving friends and family provide a valuable reality check to young couples. Never an arbitrary downer, these insights naturally corrects the tendencies toward isolation which can destroy marriages before they begin!

I realized that I needed to ask this couple a question that I now ask all engaged couples. To date I have asked this question to over 400 couples, and their responses to this question have changed the way we offer marriage preparation. Here is the original question broken down into its parts:

⋄ "Do you admire your parents' marriage, and would you be happy if you had a marriage like theirs?" The majority of the couples respond, "no."
⋄ "Do you know of a married couple whose marriage you admire, and would you be happy if your marriage was like theirs?" Almost every time, they answer an emphatic "yes!"
⋄ "Is this couple a part of your lives? Do they share their marriage with you?" They usually answer that while this couple is part of their lives to some extent, they wish for a closer relationship.

Over time, the reality of this disconnect hit me. These couples were isolated not because they wanted to be, but because they didn't know how to connect with those couples whom they admired! With the exception of those few couples who admired their parents' marriage, the majority of young couples were looking at others' marriages from afar, often in an unhealthy and idolizing way, and with no clear avenue for imitating them.

Those married couples were living out their wedding vows, day in and day out, making mistakes and asking for forgiveness. They started each day anew attempting to love their spouses in the way that God intended. They had no idea that other young couples in their community looked up to them. They had no idea that an isolated, young, engaged couple not only needed but craved a small conversation, a deeper friendship with another couple. These engaged couples desired community, fellowship, support, and an organic mentorship. Organic mentorship, so vital to healthy marriages, was more prominent in past generations but today has become a luxury.

In today's culture, the young couple who admires from afar needs permission to ask another married couple to be a part of their lives. They need them to walk alongside to the altar and beyond. Ultimately, they need you to become an inspiration and a measure of reality. You are called to pray for them, laugh with them, and to connect them to their church, to the wider community, and to God.

How do we solve the "disconnect dilemma?" As I asked the same question over and over, the challenge these couples faced weighed on me. Did we need a "program" to make something so natural happen? How could I convince engaged couples to approach the married couple they admired and simply ask them to be their mentors? It was like telling a boy that he should walk up to the prettiest girl in the class and ask her out. No way!

I assured the engaged couples that no married couple would reject them if approached with these sentiments: "We admire your marriage. We want what you have. Please share your marriage with us. Please walk with us." Why? When the married couple is asked to be a mentor, all that is good in their marriage is recognized and all that is imperfect blushes and wants to run away, but doesn't. The mentor sees the need in a young couple's eyes and say, "Yes!" Throughout the process of becoming mentors, what is good in their marriage is strengthened, and those areas of deficiency are admitted and shared.

While I encouraged many couples to reach out and consider asking that couple whom they admired to be mentors, I knew deep down that the majority would not ask. Eventually, I began working part-time at a small country church that had a mentor marriage preparation program. I thought that, at last, engaged couples would have the support they needed. Eventually, we saw that engaged couples would meet with their parish assigned mentors, but they would not connect in a way that would give them the support they needed over the years.

One day we heard that a couple with whom we had worked, who had gone through all the requirements and had met for months with their well-formed mentors, was now divorced. Their mentors never knew. The engaged couple never established a trusting relationship with them and did not approached them during their difficulty.

I then realized that trust and friendship are the keys to true marriage mentorship. Trust is the bridge needed to make successful marriage preparation possible. The most important conversations require trust and established relationships. Did we need another "program" to make it all happen?!? What would that program look like? How would we know if it was working? Father Michael Delcambre, Pastor of St. Joseph & St. Rose Parish in Cecilia, Louisiana, and I prayed over and discussed what this would look like. We decided to try it out on our next couple.

We provided guidelines and training, but ultimately we let them choose their own mentor couple. We gave them questions to discuss together, worksheets on communication and finances, tips for great conversations, and a "Scavenger Hunt List" that kept everyone on track. This list included many practical things that engaged couples needed to do, but it was also focused on enhancing the relationship between the two couples. It was about breaking down the isolation prevalent even in those relationships.

> Trust and friendship are the keys to true marriage mentorship. Trust is the bridge needed to make successful marriage preparation possible.

This process grew and strengthened over the years, and in 2014 we were asked to present this program, called "Witness to Love," as a simple workshop at the conference for the National Association of Catholic Family Life Ministers. The overwhelming interest that emerged from this presentation prompted us to write a training manual. The conference experience also prompted the humbling invitation to write this book.

5

It may take many years before churches around the world realize that the enriching of marriage preparation through couple mentoring is one of the keys to the renewal of marriage and the family. This renewal begins with smallest healing glimpse, a simple invitation into the world of healthy married couples. Some things start best when they start small. Those couples who have never experienced healthy family life will find even the merest exposure to it an inspiration.

You can begin tearing down the wall of isolation that surrounds young couples today when you invite them into your homes, families, and lives and when you share the gift of your marriage with them. The expression "you only get to keep what you give away" is never truer than when describing a mentor couple who shares the riches and blessings of their own relationship. A priest told us recently that while there are many couples with beautiful marriages, too often their example is hidden away. He said that the doors of many "domestic churches" are closed, but he noticed that our door was open because we shared our marriage, home, and lives with others. What a compliment. We hope that after reading this book you would consider opening wide the doors to your domestic church!

Chapter 1

A State of Dis-Union: The Divorce Effect

Marriage Defined

WE live in a state of "Dis-Union." The word "marriage" has been slowly separated from its original meaning. God is not part of the wedding vows. Couples choose to "share a residence" rather than build a permanent home. The tragedy of divorce has left an ugly scar on the heart of marriage. Marriage, the "one blessing not forfeited by original sin, nor washed away by the flood,"[1] has been the crown of civilization since the very beginning. For thousands of years marriage has been a sacred starting point in the new life that a couple shares together. Marriage is a reflection of the permanence of God's covenant with us: ". . . so great a mystery that in the wedding covenant you foreshadowed the Sacrament of Christ and His Church."[2] Marriage is meant to be sacred, permanent, and beautiful. It is a reflection of God's love for us. It is an image of the Trinity. It is an opportunity to share your life at the deepest level possible with another human person. It is an invitation to sanctity and self-sacrifice. Marriage is the cradle for welcoming new life into the world. It is the domestic church in which we teach our children and family about God. It is our path to Heaven. It is "for better or for worse, in sickness and in health." Marriage is an amazing blessing!

Battle-weary couples struggle to live out God's plan for this "one blessing." We find at every click of a mouse and scrolling of a page some subtle opposition to this blessing that even original sin and the flood could not destroy. We are living in a time in history during which both the beauty and the acceptance of the permanence of marriage are collapsing into disarray. We certainly see "dis-union" in the tragedy of divorce, but also we encounter it in the understanding and living out of married life.

Marriage has borne the brunt of every sordid sitcom satire, and has unwillingly become a hot political pawn. Pope St. John Paul II prophetically said, "As the family goes, so goes the nation, and so goes the whole world in which we live."[3] Look at our families, our nation, and our world today. When married couples forget what marriage is really about it should be no surprise that the definition of marriage is "updated" to become more inclusive. If we do not protect the meaning of marriage by living out our own marriages with purpose, then we should not be surprised when it's emptied of real meaning and subsequently used for political agendas.

The word "marriage" comes from the Latin word "matrimonium" which means "the state of becoming a mother." Today, the very word marriage points to no abiding reality nor to its original intelligibility. Its true meaning is no longer considered "politically correct." Having children is an optional part of marriage. A man can be a "mother," or a woman can decide to be a "father." I may be forgetting some other variations, but suffice it to say that today marriage means as many different things as the number of people you ask. The meaning of marriage, and the definition of family as well, suffer tremendous assault. How can we expect couples who do not even understand the meaning of marriage to be able to form a healthy family? No wonder there is so much confusion!

Here is another example of the "dis-union" that we see in marriage today. God, the Author of Marriage, has been removed from the relationship

⬦

If we do not protect the meaning of marriage by living out our own marriages with purpose, then we should not be surprised when it's emptied of real meaning and subsequently used for political agendas.

⬦

between man and woman to the point where oftentimes any reference to God is removed from the wedding vows. Some couples write their own vows; and as sweet as that is, they are often not promising each other the same things found in traditional wedding vows. The wedding vow should include a marital promise of: permanence, fidelity, obedience, mutual help, and openness to life between one man and one woman. Consider yourself fortunate if you hear more than one of these promises in the personal vows recited at so many contemporary weddings.

Such weddings often exclude God and any sense of sacred is obscured. Whereas the focus should be on presenting yourselves to God and to your community, and having your vows to God and to each other received by a witness (the priest, deacon or pastor), very often the focus and theme highlights a couple's love for each other *without* the help of God. The "vows" make no reference to how they will witness God's love to each other and to their family. This "vow" is a contract; it is *not* a sacrament. A contract is an exchange of goods and services over a period of time that can be negotiated or terminated if one party fails to fulfill their obligations.

A sacrament, by comparison, involves a pledge that goes beyond an obligation. In a sacramental marriage vow you abide, for the rest of your life, by an oath made between you and your spouse and between you as a couple and God. It is not a negative restriction but an oath that opens up the door to give of yourself freely and totally. Unlike a contract—which is about limitations, expectations, and rules—a sacrament is an oath or a covenant that provides an environment of giving of yourself beyond restrictions. It is a commitment that cannot be broken, and treating it as merely a contract risks eternal disappointment.

The Cohabitation Effect

So many young couples today are choosing to cohabit rather than present themselves for the sacrament of marriage or even the civil contract of marriage. Why is this the case? Can we really blame them? Perhaps the touted 50 percent divorce rate scares them off. Perhaps they do not believe in sacraments and the grace they bestow. Perhaps their parents were divorced and they fear commitment. It is very easy for couples to linger outside the sacrament of marriage and to settle for a "social marriage" or "romantic partnership" because they truly do not know what they are missing. Who is reaching out to them and sharing the quiet, transforming love of the sacrament of marriage? Who is helping to strengthen marriages that are struggling? Who is preaching the good news that the majority of first time marriages *do* in fact make it?[4] Studies show that the number one reason for cohabitation is "fear of divorce,"[5] but cohabitation only leads to more divorce![6]

> A sacrament is an oath or a covenant that provides an environment of giving of yourself beyond restrictions. It is a commitment that cannot be broken, and treating it as merely a contract risks eternal disappointment.

When discussing cohabitation with young couples, it is a challenge not to paint them into a corner by immediately judging their decision to live together. We must not evaluate their actions based on our understanding of right and wrong. Many cohabiting couples don't understand why anyone would think what they are doing is less than good. Many parents support the decision to cohabit because they think it is important for their kids to make sure this is the "right one" or that they are "compatible."

I (Mary-Rose) remember one summer spent with a family in Germany. They had a son and a daughter. The son had a boyfriend, and they disapproved of the relationship but would not say anything. The daughter lived with her

11

boyfriend for seven years, and the parents said that they would pay for her wedding only if she made it to ten years. The issue was not that they disliked him, but their fifty years of marriage taught them that it was very hard to tolerate each other, and they wanted to make sure their daughter knew what she was getting into. In the nineties this philosophy seemed laissez-faire, but now it is simply commonplace. Marriage rates are falling, and cohabitation rates are going up.[7] Statistics also indicate that divorce rates have plateaued or even started to decrease.[8] If divorce rates truly are falling, the most likely cause is the increase in cohabitation and not that marriages are getting stronger or lasting longer.

In other words, as cohabitation rates go up around the world divorce rates will fall. This is not because marriage has been tried and found good but because fewer couples are finding their way to the altar. Couples today will tell you that cohabiting is no big deal and that most couples do it. Statistics show that over 60 percent of couples who get married have cohabited prior to marriage. Eight percent of the U.S. population is currently in a "cohabiting relationship." This is no small number!

Think about those couples you know who are cohabiting. Think about their children, jobs, finances, families, and faith. Often, they always seem to be just getting by. They are more isolated from those couples who could share the witness of what marriage is all about. These couples, more than other couples you know, need your witness of the gift and permanence of marriage! Is this just about trying to convince all those couples we know who are cohabiting to get married? Not necessarily. The fact that the majority of engaged couples are sexually active can cause us to lose focus on what these couples need to learn about marriage and themselves. Instead of working with these couples, we frequently try to ensure that those who are cohabiting get married A.S.A.P.! This does not help anyone. Instead, we should encourage deeper conversations with these couples so that they can fully understand the "more" that is there for them—the gift of married life and love.

The point is to love everyone we know so that they can see a little glimpse of God in us and to help them to see a future full of the hope that God has in store for them. Often cohabiting situations present a couple with an unfounded belief that there is nothing else for them. In some cases they see marriage as an impossibility, which makes it even more important that they develop a relationship with a couple whose marriage can help to inspire and encourage them. Sharing the gift of your witness with those who are disillusioned and caught in a fear of failure is needed to combat the many moral and marital tragedies displayed today.

The Question of Divorce

Lest you think the urgency of what you are reading is unfounded, we will dedicate the rest of this chapter to a simple "State of the Union" or rather "Dis-Union" with regards to marriage. While the divorce rate seems to have slowed down and perhaps even changed direction,[9] the esteem for marriage is at an all time low. Even those who have good marriages live in fear of losing theirs because of the rampant tragedy of divorce. This is due in part to the frequently cited divorce rate of more than 50 percent that everyone seems to know, and it is also due to the number of friends and family we see going through divorce.

If you think about it for a minute, you will realize that 50 percent of the people you know probably are not divorced. You may then wonder where that 50 percent divorce rate comes from. Even many of those conducting the studies are in disagreement. The fact of the matter is that the divorce rate peaked around 50 percent (some would say it peaked at 41 percent)[10] back in the late seventies after "no-fault divorce" was declared. However, a couple's backgrounds and choices are very distinct factors that determine their chance of divorce. It is far more helpful and effective to focus on understanding and battling the main indicators for divorce rather than wringing our hands over generalities or stressing out over which statistic is most accurate.

Those vague studies that we just assume are accurate begin to weigh heavily on us. That often-quoted 50 percent divorce rate has done its damage. If you try to play a game that seems impossible, then how hard will you really try? For example, if I am a terrible Scrabble player, I go into the game knowing I will lose. I do not enjoy the game, I do not get passionately into it, and yes, I usually lose. This is what that haunting 50 percent divorce rate quote does to many couples. It condescendingly mocks, "If you don't make it, that's okay. Most won't make it." Or, "When you feel like it won't work out, don't think you are the only ones." Do you see what this does to a couple's marital morale? On what should couples be focusing? They should know the key indicators for divorce; work to resolve those issues; seek help or mentorship from those who are skilled in those areas; develop a game plan for solving and discussing those issues; and most importantly, ask God to reveal the plan He has for their relationship.

We were greatly relieved the first time we saw a study done on seven predictors of divorce dealing simply with the wedding. The study showed, for example, that those who were together for more than two years, had large, inexpensive weddings, went on a honeymoon, made enough money, and bought a decent engagement ring (not the cheapest one on the display) had much higher chances of marital permanence than those who had a small or expensive wedding. When we read this study, we felt that a weight had been lifted. Why? Because we had been good friends for two years before we dated, we had a great many friends and family at our wedding, but we did not break the bank, and we went on a honeymoon to Mexico. We thought we were just doing what we "preferred." In retrospect, all those choices became indicators that pointed towards a marriage deeply rooted in a community of support and friendship. Studies show that couples who are supported by a wide group of friends and family are more likely to succeed and flourish.[11]

Returning to the Scrabble analogy, there was a time when Mary-Rose was invited to play with a group and was told that there was one person playing that "always lost." So she played hard, and thoroughly enjoyed coming in "next to last." Even though she came in next to last she was only a few points behind the friend who came in second. Not "losing" when it comes to marriage is just as good as winning, but you have to play *and* stay in the game! Studies show that, even if you are in a challenging marriage now, if you decide to stick it out and work on your issues, you will be happily married five years from now.[12] How many couples do you know who experienced huge challenges, even infidelity, and are happily married now? We know many. Why? Because they were not afraid to share their stories with us, to be vulnerable, to give credit to God's love and mercy, and to witness to the love and the hard work that it takes to stay in the game!

Predisposed for Divorce

Young couples who are not aware that there are specific factors that indicate a higher or lower chance of divorce will simply assume that they have a 50 percent chance of divorce. This is not the case! They may have a 10 percent chance or a 90 percent chance. To tell them that their chance of divorce is 50 percent without looking at their specific indicators would be a missed opportunity to strengthen a future marriage! So many couples say that divorce "happens" to someone as if they caught a disease. Yes, divorce does "happen" to many couples, but as we have shared, they are not simply victims of a tragedy.

An important analogy comparing the different ways that couples view their increased risk of marital failure can be made by comparing the following approach of two men whose families have a history of heart disease. The first man knows that his grandfather died from heart disease. He knows that because of his background and personal decisions, he himself has high blood pressure and cholesterol.

He now knows that it is important for him to live a healthy lifestyle, and he sees his doctor regularly and checks in if something out of the ordinary happens. He keeps himself educated and informed on ways to recognize signs of a heart attack. He surrounds himself with those who will encourage and support his change of lifestyle. With the proper care, self-determination, awareness and support he will outlive his projected years.

The second man knows that men in his family have a history of heart disease, but he tries not to let that get him down. When his time comes, it comes. No use fretting over something he can't change. He lives life as if he did not have a higher risk for heart disease. Tragically and without warning he has a heart attack and dies young. Yes, it is a tragedy, and yes, it was unexpected, but it could have been prevented! In comparing the two men and their approaches to the way that they handled the reality of their predisposition to heart disease, we can see a correlation in the ways that couples with a predisposition for marital "heart disease" often approach the issue. "Heart disease" in marriage causes the tragedy of divorce, but in most cases it could have been avoided!

If couples with a predisposition for marital heart disease change their lifestyle, get help regularly, stay educated and informed, and know how to recognize an issue before it gets bad, they will have a much higher chance of marital success. Most importantly, if they stay surrounded by those who support them, their marriage will live to a ripe old age, and they will celebrate 50, 60, or even 70 years of marriage. Their witness will strengthen their family for generations to come.

They will change the statistics and turn the tide, but they need your help to get there. If they continue to live unsupported and uninformed, their marriages will die young, and this will impact their future generations, and their children's chances of having healthy marriages.

There are two main kinds of studies about marriage and divorce. The first looks at the "red-flags" that can be noticed *prior* to marriage and how those issues can be remedied. The second looks at the potential "red flags" that can be seen *in marriage* and how couples can prevent becoming a statistic.

The standard approach that most studies on divorce take is that they look for clues that a tragedy was more likely to happen based on the presence of the following in already divorced couples:

◇ certain personal traits
◇ experiences
◇ decisions or family of origin dynamics

These are examined for each partner individually and then considered collectively to determine a couple's statistical chances of divorce or success.

Other studies focus on the following:

◇ an individual's chances of divorce
◇ a couple's chances of divorce
◇ indicators for divorce that occurred prior to marriage
◇ situations, reactions, events, or decisions made in marriage that increase chances of divorce or increase marital satisfaction.

For your mentoring purposes, we will cover those "red flags" that can be noted prior to marriage as indicators for a higher risk of divorce in Chapter Seven: Mentoring the "Unmarried." We will cover those additional "red flags" that can be noted as causes for divorce once you are already married in Chapter Eight: After "I Do": Continuing the Mentorship.

Chapter 2

Do You Have What It Takes?

Life Changing Words

WE would like to share an important event in our past. It was on a cold field in Toronto, Canada that we each heard for the first time the words from a wise man that would change our lives. His words would challenge and encourage us to become witnesses to the love of Christ in our lives, despite our own fears and failures. We have all failed both in our personal lives and in our family life, but there is nothing that can keep us from the love of God's healing.

The event was World Youth Day in July of 2002. The wise man was Pope Saint John Paul II. Recently, we discovered that while we would not meet for three more years, on this night Ryan and I were on the same field listening to the words of our beloved pope. We sometimes reflect on the time that we each sat with a different group under the same sky asking God to show us where He wanted us in life and what we needed to heal. Over the years, we have read and reread the message that Pope Saint John Paul II imparted to the hundreds of thousands of young people gathered on that Toronto field. We have discussed and prayed over those words because in many ways that night was a starting point for each of us. We would like to share some of this pope's words with you. We share it in the hope that you too might see things in a new light—the healing light of Christ's love for you and the need to for you to share that healing light with others.

> The world you are inheriting is a world which desperately needs a new sense of brotherhood and human solidarity. It is a world which needs to be touched and healed by the beauty and richness of God's love. *It needs witnesses to that love. The world needs salt. It needs you*– to be the salt of the earth and the light of the world.[1]

Our world is disconnected and our sense of "brotherhood" is in desperate need of renewal. We live in such a transient, fast-paced world that it is hard to believe that true community is possible. Relationships wherein we are able to share our true selves without fear of judgment or abandonment are relationships wherein we experience God's love. True community is like Heaven. We rejoice in God's presence with those who love us and love Him. In Heaven we have nothing to hide and nothing to fear. It is through relationships of love, brotherhood, and solidarity this that the world will be "touched and healed" through YOU and ME. You are called to witness to love. Young couples desperately need your witness. Your spouse needs this witness. We need your witness.

These were the final words of Pope John Paul II's exhortation to us that day: "*We are not the sum of our weaknesses and failures*; we are the sum of the Father's love for us and our real capacity to become the image of his Son."[2] As we each sat in our separate groups with our little radios transmitting the Pope's message, his final words knocked over the walls we had put up in our hearts. The excuses we had made to distance ourselves from God's plan for us no longer stood. There are no other words that could have had a deeper impact on our lives.

Before these final words we were just enjoying World Youth Day and all the excitement of meeting new people from every corner of the earth, singing, and dancing. It was like a massive block party. After these final words I (Mary-Rose) looked up at the sky with tears streaming down my face. I sat in the field for what seemed like an eternity. "How could God love someone as broken as me? How could He use me with all my mistakes, broken family life, and distorted view of who God is? How could He accept me with my scarred idea of marriage, my pride and fears, and most of all the wounds that I bore in my soul from so many who had hurt me over the years? I wept at the disconnect between the place where I thought I was and the place where God ultimately wanted me to be. I had to face my weakness and God's strength, my fears and God's love, my emptiness and His fullness, my deep need to know a Father's love and His claim to be my perfect Father. For the first time a river of hope ran through me. I knew without a doubt that I had a Father who loved me. That was enough. That is all we ever really need to know to make life worth living both for ourselves and for others. If you know the Father's love for you, then you have what it takes!

Mentoring: Intentional Sharing

By sharing this story, we hope to illustrate that this book is about more than simply beating the divorce statistic. This book is about love, grace, healing, reverence for marriage, and seeing God's love in the way you and your spouse love each other. This chapter will help you to identify what needs to grow in your marriage to nourish your relationship so you can share those strengths with others.

> I had to face my weakness and God's strength, my fears and God's love, my emptiness and His fullness, my deep need to know a Father's love and His claim to be my perfect Father.

The question at hand is not "Is your marriage good enough to share?" but rather "Are you able to identify what is best in your marriage and how you got there?" *and* "What is still in need of improvement and do you have what it takes to grow in those areas?" Not only must you ask yourselves if you have what it takes to grow your marriage, but also are you humble enough to share both the things you are proud of and the things you are not so proud of in your marriage? Both the positive and negative aspects of your relationship are part of your marriage. If you share only what you desire to be seen, you falsely represents all of the hard work that goes into marriage! Earlier we discussed the need for married couples who can invite engaged and newly-married couples into the reality of marriage. The invitation to understand the daily struggles that come with marriage is not only divorce insurance for young couples, it is also an opportunity to grow in your own marriage.

In our experience in working with mentor couples and engaged couples we have seen beautiful fruits in the marriages of the mentor couples as they learn to share their marriages with the engaged couples. Each time we enter the process of teaching mentors about how to share their marriage, we hear a version of these sentiments:

> When we were chosen to mentor, we were so surprised to know that another couple admired our marriage. We thought we were just an average couple with the same struggles as any other couple. However, knowing that we have to work with an engaged couple who admires our relationship has helped us to work on our marriage. We want to share our marriage with them even though it is not perfect and we want to do better as a couple!

We are touched and encouraged when it is communicated to us that someone else would like to have a marriage like ours. Some may wonder if it is realistic that engaged couples would communicate to married couples that they see their marriage as a model? The answer is YES!

Why shouldn't we strive to support couples preparing for marriage with an example of a couple attempting to live what Christ intended within the sacrament of matrimony? We could focus on what we still need to work on in our relationship, and use this as an excuse to do nothing; or, we could acknowledge what needs perfecting and start working on it. It is good to let engaged couples know that you are not perfect. No marriage is perfect. This insight is key to knowing how and what you will share. If you idealize married life, you do engaged couples no service. Instead, share what is real and let them know about those areas in your marriage that you are working on. This is the invitation to view the reality of committed self-sacrifice, that cohabitating and engaged married couples need to see. They do not need to see the "finished product." The key is to paint a real picture of married life to help them understand the processes that enable couples to celebrate major anniversary milestones in marriage. Without the real witness of love lived out, how will they come to understand the depth of marriage, and the joy and security of a shared life lived in God?

> If you idealize married life, you do engaged couples no service. Instead, share what is real and let them know about those areas in your marriage that you are working on. This is the invitation to view the reality of committed self-sacrifice, that cohabitating and engaged married couples need to see.

Every day each of us shares our marriages with others either intentionally or unintentionally. Before you consider "intentionally sharing" your marriage with others, take inventory of where you are in your own marriage. Here are some questions to discuss with your spouse as you begin praying about sharing the gift of your marriage with others. These questions will also help you to identify what areas of your marriage may already be an inspiration to others:

- ◇ What season of marriage are you in? (young children, teens, empty nest)
- ◇ What do you consider to be the best aspects of your marriage?
  - o your ability to communicate
  - o your kindness to each other
  - o the struggles you have survived together
  - o the healing that has taken place in your relationship
  - o the way your kids turned out
  - o the blessing of praying together
  - o the way you understand what the other needs
  - o how you handle finances together
  - o your reverence for the gift of sexuality in your marriage
  - o the way you handle everyday life and roles around the house
  - o something uniquely your own that is not listed here[3]

In your conversation focus on what is good in your lives or the aspects of your life together for which you are most grateful. These are the crowning jewels of your relationship. These are the works of art that others see and admire in you. Thank God for these gifts that He has given you and ask Him to bless and multiply these aspects of your lives. These areas should be kept in mind as we discuss how to share your marriage in the subsequent chapters. Take a moment now to write your thoughts down. In upcoming chapters we will discuss specifically how to share these gifts with those you mentor and how to obtain key insights into specific areas of your relationship that are most helpful in your sharing your journey. This is an important part of "intentional mentoring."

You are the Perfect "Imperfect" Couple

Now look at the areas of your relationship that seem to be a daily struggle. This includes those areas of disunity and selfishness that creep into your lives. We would all like to pretend that they don't exist and that those occasional outbursts that cut your spouse to the quick are not part your marriage. These issues create nagging doubts that prevent you from sharing the true reality of your marriage, and they cause you to think: "How can I ever help anyone when my relationship is just a mess?" Do not dismiss all that is good and beautiful in your relationship because of the areas in which you are growing! Good marriages take a long time and a lot of work from *both* spouses. If you wait to share what is good in your relationship until you are both perfect in all areas then you will most likely forget how you got there in the first place. Why wait to save your perfect marriage to witness to the nursing home staff when the rest of us are missing out on the fruits of your labors today!

Here are a few examples of areas that married couples often struggle with:

⋄ outbursts of disrespect
⋄ talking about your spouse behind his/her back
⋄ constant disagreements over parenting
⋄ causing division between your spouse and his/her family (adding to the in-law drama)
⋄ too many distractions while in your spouse's presence (technology or work)
⋄ a lack of respect for your spouse's dignity or yours (pornography or steamy romance novels)
⋄ financial secretiveness from your spouse
⋄ overspending your energy without saving some for your spouse
⋄ belittling each other
⋄ forgetful of your vows to "love, honor and cherish"
⋄ not being on the same page when it comes to your relationship with God (one spouse "dragging" the other along)
⋄ not dedicating time to be together as a couple (date nights, prayer, fun)
⋄ overly separate lives, careers, hobbies, or friends
⋄ tuning out your spouse and their needs
⋄ holding on to hurt and resentment

Young couples need to know the struggles that those with the "perfect" relationship actually have. They do need to know *what* you are struggling with and that you have a game plan to work on these issues.

If you want to save marriages identify first what is good in your marriage *and* how you got there, and *then* identify what needs to grow and your game plan for making it happen. Take some time to discuss with your spouse things such as:

◇ Do we need marital counseling?

◇ Should we pray together more?

◇ Do we need to confide in another couple who seem to have strengths in an area in which we need to grow?

◇ Do we need to go to confession (if Catholic) and seek counsel from a pastor or priest?

You may be thinking, "We are a mess. We'll never be able to be mentors." I want to state here that those couples who:

◇ are honest about where they need to grow

◇ develop a plan to get there

◇ hold one another accountable

◇ confide in another person or couple who can help

◇ ask God to help you do better

will become those mentor couples that the world needs.

A Marriage Restoration Project

Your marriage relationship is like a priceless masterpiece from which some paint has begun to peel and upon which small cracks have begun to form. Every marriage needs some occasional restoration. Your marriage is a work of art more beautiful that the most valuable paintings created by the greatest artists in the world. Millions of dollars are spent on fixing the cracks in the Sistine Chapel, preserving frescos shattered during earthquakes, and removing the carbon from the ancient Greek statues. Is your marriage not worth more than these? If not, then you are selling your masterpiece for far less than it is worth! Your marriage is an image of God, the greatest artist of all. He is the One to whom you should look as you seek to recreate your masterpiece. God has a design for your marriage. He wants your marriage to be an image of His love and His plan for you. God will hear the prayer of a husband and wife who gather in His name and ask Him to reveal His plan for their marriage. God wants a future for you full of hope, joy, and love with your spouse in the way that you were created to be. Your spouse should be revealing to you how God loves you. Anything less is selling yourself short, your spouse short, and your Heavenly Father short!

So when is your marriage going to be "good enough" to share with others? This is not a simple question with a simple answer. You are sharing your marriage all the time, either intentionally or unintentionally. Examples of intentional sharing of your marriage are:

◇ offering to be a mentor couple at your parish
◇ telling family and friends they can send their adult children to you to discuss marital struggles
◇ being open with your own teens or adult children about the beauty and the ugliness of marriage
◇ inviting others to attend retreats or presentations for married couples

◇ reading and sharing good books on marriage and family life.

All of these are great ways to intentionally share your marriage. As you begin to share, do not be surprised when your flaws are magnified right before your eyes. I say *when*, and not *if*, because it will happen. You will cringe and want to forget about ever sharing your imperfections with anyone. But then something amazing will happen. Any complacency or stagnant aspect of your relationship that needs deep cleansing and healing will be brought into the light. Resolve now to not give up and not give in to dismissing those highlighted areas of your relationship with God, spouse, or family that need to grow and to heal! Your relationship will grow in your preparation to share it all. Your imperfections will gradually be touched by God's grace, and His and your love will be more than able to restore your marriage to the original plan that God has for it.

> Let your home become the mission field, and let your marriage become your apostolate. Let your domestic church become a missionary outpost of your local church!

Do not wait to be a perfect couple in a perfect marriage before you feel that you have something to offer. Let your home become the mission field, and let your marriage become your apostolate. Let your domestic church become a missionary outpost of your local church! Remember, you are the perfect "imperfect" couple.

Chapter 3

Who Has Time for Mentoring?

Make the Time to Share your Blessings

EVEN the best of couples are busy and focused on important things like family, children's education, work, exercise, doctor's appointments, fundraisers, parties, shopping, reading, cleaning, social media. . . . the list is endless. We barely have time for ourselves let alone our spouse and kids! And you want us to take on something else?

Before you throw this book at your spouse, take a deep breath, and consider the following:

◇ Has anyone ever reached out to you and mentored you or your marriage even in a small way?
◇ How many minutes does it take to change someone's life?
◇ Who has God put in your life and how have you responded to their need?
◇ Is there a an aspect of your daily life that seems important but is too time-consuming?

⋄ Do you need to make more time for God in your life together?

⋄ What do you feel called to share with other couples?

⋄ How has God healed your marriage?

If we have been blessed with a happy marriage, an understanding of God's plan for married love, and strong parenting skills, then we will have to give God an account of how we used our talents. It is not enough just to work on having a great marriage! Again let us say, *If you wait for your marriage to be perfect before you share what is already worth sharing in your marriage, you will miss being able to impact many lives!*

Getting Serious about Intentional Mentoring

So if you have never thought about sharing your marriage, please think about it. Remember that you are always sharing your marriage, either intentionally or unintentionally. Why not intentionally share the best of what you have, rather than unintentionally sharing the worst of what you have? Is it really that much work to do something with intentionality? Well, yes, it is more work! But that does not mean that it will take more of your time. Consider these two paths to get ready to run a marathon:

Path one. You tell friends, co-workers, and acquaintances that you are going to run. They give you their two cents, a few tips or cautions. You start to run a bit more than you already are (pull a few muscles and figure it is just part of the process), watch what you eat, get excited about the race, and really hope you do well. You put a lot of time and energy into getting ready, but you lack a good mentor or trainer. You run, but you come in close to last. You are not sure you will ever run another marathon and your knee might be shot.

Path two. You seek out people who have run a marathon before, and get some tips and sound advice from them. You get a fitness trainer, log your progress, track what you eat, research what you should eat, work on specific muscle groups, and run a terrain similar to where you will actually run. You find a friend to run with you, spot each other, and begin to train together. The day comes and you are excited and confident because you know you did what it takes to prepare well. It is quite possible that you spent less time preparing for the race than the person who took path one—the unintentional path.

Intentionality is hard work but often it takes less time and produces more accurate, productive, intended results. You know what you need to do, how to get there, and who you need to help you accomplish your goals.

Apply the same concept to mentoring.

Path one: unintentional mentoring. You may know a couple or two who look up to you. They may ask you questions, and you may give them off-handed, poorly thought out responses, without consulting your spouse for input. You may feel like you are giving them something helpful, and perhaps you are. They may have quite a few friends giving them random advice. They sort through it and put it all together. Some of it may conflict, but overall it is a good collection of input from friends and acquaintances. They may put some of it into practice.

Path two: intentional mentoring. You know a couple who admires your marriage. You discuss this with your spouse. Before you consider "intentionally sharing" your marriage with others, it is important to take inventory of where you are in your own marriage. You both agree to talk to a relationship "coach" or counselor. This way you can work through any issues you have as a couple that would be better addressed by going this route. You pray together so that God might reveal what needs to grow and heal in your marriage. You pray for those couples whom you have invited into your home. You intentionally work on your marriage for the sake of your relationship, and you also focus on how you got there, so that you might help others. You reach out to the young couple who admires your marriage, invite them into your lives, and share the fruits of your relationship with them. You remember, of course, the discussion questions in Chapter 2, and you recall those gems of wisdom that you can now offer. This is intentional mentoring. Does it take more time? Yes, but the payoff is worth it. Is it more work? Anything that is worthwhile takes more effort. Will you benefit from it? Absolutely! Do you have an obligation or a responsibility to share your marriage? If you remember the Parable of the Talents, you may have also have pondered the phrase, "Those to whom much has been given, much will be required."[1] A paraphrase would be, "If you have a great marriage, please do not keep it to yourself."

We are our Neighbor's Keeper

If we do not care enough about the future marriages of those around us to show a little extra concern and kindness towards them, then are we living as we should? We will know one day whose lives we've touched for the good. So what if "I'm not a people person" or "I'm too busy" or "I don't have a minute for myself!" God can move mountains in your marriage and in others' marriages through you, if you give Him an hour or two. Don't feel like this is a phone solicitation with someone trying to sell you cookies, knives, or some gadget you don't need. See this as God gently knocking (or maybe banging hard) on the front door of your heart. He is asking you to give your marriage everything you've got. Recall that your marriage reflects God's unconditional love, and perhaps you are being called to share His love with others. It is going to take a lifetime to learn to love the way God created you to love and for you to learn how to more perfectly share that love with others.

> Recall that your marriage reflects God's unconditional love, and perhaps you are being called to share His love with others. It is going to take a lifetime to learn to love the way God created you to love and for you to learn how to more perfectly share that love with others.

However, the good news is that you do not have to wait until you are checking into a nursing home to do this. Know that you are receiving lifelong graces and gifts in your work to bring out the best in your marriage and to share it intentionally!

We hope today that you find a renewed mission to strengthen and share your marriage, and that you continue to develop an awareness of the impact a simple word or a kind gesture will have on the future marriage of another couple. If there are married couples you know who are struggling in less than joyful marriages, then reach out to them. There is nothing better than teaching something to another couple to help mentors focus on what needs growth and healing in their own marriages. It is in community and in sharing our marriage that we find our own relationship renewed. Clearly, there is an obvious need for good role models for young couples today, but more importantly, there is a need for mentors who understand the theology and practice of the domestic church, the church of the home. We must heed Christ's words to encourage us to put out into the deep and share what is dearest to us so we can be fishers of men and catch souls for Christ. Who doesn't have time for this incredible evangelizing mission!

Chapter 4

The Mentorless Generation's Need for Solidarity

The Divorce Culture

How many young hearts, still raw from broken homes, some patched up by a few short counseling sessions, are now seeking to make the promise "to love, honor and cherish 'til death do we part?" How many are able to keep that promise?

If you were told that the plane you were boarding had a 40 percent to 50 percent chance of crashing, would you get on it? We witness couples getting on the "wedding plane" every weekend at altars everywhere, and a few years later we find out that the marriage had crashed. Are there casualties? Of course. If you have ever looked into the eyes of a man or woman going through a divorce, you have seen the crash site. If you have watched children struggle to keep their broken hearts together through the years after their home is divided, then you have seen the devastation that can occur. If you have seen the old wounds resurface when a child of divorce grows up and marries and struggles in his own marriage, then you have seen the fallout that divorce causes. We can live in fear of statistics, or we can use them to conquer the divorce epidemic.

When we were first married and had survived that first year of marriage, we felt that somehow we had avoided being that divorce statistic for one year. We then thought of how many years we would have to work to dodge the "divorce bombs" that were taking out our friends one by one. It was as if a mysterious disease was silently spreading, and there was nothing we could do about it besides stand back, count the causalities, and pray it didn't attack us.

Later, after surviving five happy years of marriage and welcoming three children, we still worried that the "divorce bomb" might hit us. We both come from families where many spouses and their children have lived through the tragic experience of divorce. In some ways we feel like there exists a small culture of divorce wherein more relatives than not have suffered through the pain and damage of a failed marriage. Although we have relatives who have remained married to the same spouse, they are the exceptions. Some members of our extended family have attempted marriage four and five times. When those who should be enjoying their grandchildren are looking for their third spouse with no criticism from anyone, it feels like our culture has given up on life-long marriage. When you see marriages among your friends and family disintegrating, it can either discourage you or encourage you to fight for your marriage. For most people, unfortunately, it seems like the path of discouragement dominates.

Parental Mentoring

This book is meant to encourage you to fight the statistics. Do what only you can do in your marriage, your family, your church, your community and beyond. There is no fight more urgent than this. It is time to promote a greater understanding and acceptance of the permanence of marriage and family.

Marriage is about serving another and eventually serving "little others." It is not about me, and it is not about you. How often is *sacrificial, self-giving love* on the forefront of an engaged couple's list of expectations for marriage? Who can explain this reality with them in a way that they can hear it and not be turned off by it? This conversation can be had in a way that will encourage and invite them to embrace the way they were created to love and to serve one another. Much heartache and disappointment can be avoided if couples enter into marriage already in a conversation with one another and in dialogue with their mentors about what serving and not being served in marriage really means. This is just one of the important conversations that used to occur when parents were the natural and ideal mentors for a young couple getting married.

As the fabric of family life has become patched and frayed over the decades due to divorce and unhappy marriages, the gap has widened between parents' desire and ability to impart their marital wisdom to their adult child, and that adult child's ability to be influenced by that parental wisdom. More often than not, couples share with us their parents' supposed words of wisdom: "Marriage is hard—really hard. You will find out. When you have kids, you won't have time for each other anymore. Don't do what we did. Marriage is REALLY, REALLY hard."

This does not model what marriage is all about. Instead, it puts couples on the defensive against each other and their children. Couples are anxiously watching to make sure their children do not disrupt their relationship, and they work hard to avoid getting into a situation where marriage or children could possibly cause any hardship or undue sacrifice. No one has a conversation with them about how to be a mother or a father, or how to discern as a couple about having children and raising them.

> Much heartache and disappointment can be avoided if couples enter into marriage already in a conversation with one another and in dialogue with their mentors about what serving and not being served in marriage really means.

When engaged or newly married couples begin to face challenges, they often think to themselves, "Oh no! My marriage is on the rocks! I have a selfish spouse, too many children. My relationship is irreparable. Maybe it never was good. I am not fulfilled, and no one is worried about my own happiness other than me. I need to focus on my own happiness. I need to get out of this marriage. This was a bad idea." Instead, they should be thinking: "Here is a beautiful opportunity for sacrifice and service that are key aspects of marriage,"

Parents usually want happiness and successful marriages for their children, so why are these conversations not always helpful or effective for young couples? Consider the response we heard from hundreds of engaged couples who said they would not be happy with a marriage like their parents. There is a disconnect between what the parents said and what was received. In order for an engaged couple to hear and act on what another married couple says, they must first admire and then desire what they see in that couple's marriage.

You might be thinking, "We aren't divorced. We have a great marriage. Why wouldn't our children listen to us?" Perhaps there are many areas in which they will listen to you if you have a helpful conversation with them, but quite frankly, many of us have fallen short in many ways as parents. We may have failed to build that bridge of intimacy with our children that enables these conversations to bear fruit. Often, parents discover this too late. They may have been so focused on their child's success, school, or future that they have lost sight of the heart of their child. It can be incredibly painful for a parent to realize this fact. It can be just as painful for children, once they are adults who desire that intimate conversation with their parents, to realize that the depth of conversation they desire is just not possible. Mentorship can happen, but it is a lot of work, and it takes years to develop. By then, the son or daughter may be struggling in his or her own marriage and may need more than a parent can give. The fact is that you cannot give what you do not have.

Do not be discouraged when you cannot give your children all that they need. They need more than we can ever give. Each of us is the sum of the knowledge and experiences received from our parents, family, friends, co-workers,

> In the same way that others will serve to benefit our children, let us contribute to the Body of Christ through our own decision to share His love and support through our active and purposeful mentoring of other couples.

and mentors, both intentional and unintentional. The guidance and good your children have received from you will be combined with what will be offered through others, especially when it is intentionally shared as part of an effective mentorship.

We are all members of the Body of Christ. God's love, from the heart of Christ, offered to us through the Body of Christ is all encompassing. His protection is there for us and our children when we fall short as parents or spouses. It is offered through the other members of the Body of Christ in their example. Thank God for His protection, forgiveness and grace! For a few blessed young couples, those mentors are their parents, but many couples will need to look outside of their immediate families for guidance, support, prayers, and practical advice. In the same way that others will serve to benefit our children, let us contribute to the Body of Christ through our own decision to share His love and support through our active and purposeful mentoring of other couples.

We need witnesses and mentors, not books and teachers, when it comes to the practical aspects of marriage. Pope John Paul II said this to families:

Much more important are *living testimonies*. As Pope Paul VI observed,

"Contemporary man listens more willingly to witnesses than to teachers, and if he listens to teachers it is because they are witnesses."[1]

Mentors model solidarity and a shared vision of caring for one another in simple and sacrificial ways. Mentors can model not only how to live out their wedding vows with reference to one another, but also in reference to future children. Mentors model healthy family life and how to be resilient when struggles descend on a growing family. Marriage mentors are those credible witnesses about which Pope John Paul II speaks.

Tale of Two Families

Here is a "Tale of Two Families" to illustrate how parents' decisions affect the hearts of their children—and future generations—when it comes to their ability to be resilient in their marriages and committed to their vows. Many people involved in marriage and family ministries probably could think of two or three families they feel are striving to live a good life and pass down this commitment to successive generations.

Family One: This family embodies the good, true, and beautiful things that the Creator has designed to be passed down from the great-grandparents to the youngest grandchildren in a family. They are not a family immune from same issues that almost every family confronts. Members of this family have struggled with depression, cancer, adolescent rebellion, and have welcomed a child conceived outside of wedlock. However, for the most part, the family seems to exude a peace and a faith that all things will somehow work out for the good. What stands out even more about this family is their intimate bond with one another. There is a tangible connectedness and interdependence that binds them together in a way that proves the goodness and necessity that marriage and family offer to individuals and communities. The many generations of this family have seen and experienced the challenges, but more importantly, they have inherited the knowledge that marriage and family are goods worth fighting for and are truly the greatest of all treasures.

Family Two: This family represents many of our own family members, who gave up and gave in to mediocre ways of living out a marriage. I myself (Ryan) have seen how divorce has plagued my own family. Recently, my great-grandmother passed away. We admired her as a strong-willed, independent woman who had a very extensive number of children, grandchildren, great-grandchildren and even great-great grandchildren! However, later in life, she ended up divorcing her husband (my great-grandfather), and from that point on the divorce plague began in our family. Of her six children, five would divorce from their first spouses (including my own grandmother). My grandmother had four children among whom only one (my own parents) remained married to their first spouse. Unfortunately, the disaster continues with numerous cousins experiencing the same pain and lost years of making good memories with their spouses and children. What remains now are awkward holidays and uncomfortable birthdays from which individuals are missing, or where people avoid making eye contact with individuals on the other side of the dining room table.

I am more grateful than ever for the gift that my parents offer to us by their marital witness which grows more beautiful as the years pass. If it was not for their marriage and the grace given to us through their witness, it would be easy for me to buy into the culture of divorce and simply bail out when things get really tough. After all, isn't life really all about how happy I should feel and how fulfilled I should be?

Like Family One, we need a great deal more than our feelings and subjective personal experiences to guide us over the rocky roads that lie ahead for every couple. If we are relying solely on our feelings and experiences, we should brace ourselves for heartache and confusion. Those without mentors can drift and struggle to find the sense of stability needed to stay firm to their commitment to remain dedicated to their wedding vows and to their family lives. When couples are faced with inevitable challenging periods and struggle to remain in a marriage because their spouse seems more like a stranger or adversary than a companion or gift, it is during these times that having a mentor to talk to could offer encouragement and save a marriage. Otherwise, they may make a few visits to a counselor who may simply tell them, "You are obviously unhappy. For the sake of your personal happiness and fulfillment, divorce is the only option. See you in two weeks after you have had time to discuss. Oh, that will be $120."

This mentorless generation desperately needs witnesses of sacrificial and enduring marital love. Most couples need mentors more than they need counselors. Those of us born anytime between the late 1960s and the early 1990s bore the brunt of the "wisdom gap." We often did not have the close relationship with grandparents that may have been common in the past, especially if our parents had remarried. When a couple divorces, not only do the children lose their parents, they often also lose the close relationship they could have had with their grandparents. We see a trend with the couples with whom we work. Many who were born in the 1990s not only have parents who are divorced, but also have grandparents who were divorced! The natural mode of marital mentorship has been damaged or irreparably destroyed in many cases. In the past, we usually heard some version of this scenario: "My parents were divorced so I don't see much that I would admire or want to bring into my future marriage, but we really look to his grandparents for those things we admire." Now, with increasing frequency we hear, "My parents are divorced, and so are her parents. Holidays are so complicated, and I really do not want that for our kids. What a strain the holidays are going to be on our kids!" These adult children who are in relationships have only negative examples to point to and say, "I know clearly what I do not want, and I vaguely know what

> Now, with increasing frequency we hear, "My parents are divorced, and so are her parents. Holidays are so complicated, and I really do not want that for our kids. What a strain the holidays are going to be on our kids!"

I do want, but I have no idea how to get there." Couples need mentors!

We can't take lightly the subtle ways that couples state and restate their unmet desire to see a model of married love that they can point to, and say, "There it is! There is someone living out marriage in a way that I admire and desire for myself." Even when they find a couple whom they do admire, they do not have an avenue for inviting them into their lives as mentors, witnesses, and friends. This is unfortunate. Every individual has an innate desire to experience a lifelong union with another person, but the path to how that desire is fulfilled and lived out in marriage is currently a very lonely and confusing path. Even if you do find your "soul mate," there will be many days and hours wasted "sweating the small stuff" and ignoring the elephant in the room.

The Art of Marriage Mentoring

How do we bridge the "wisdom gap" of marital mentoring? How do we find credible witnesses whom the "mentorless generation" will trust and turn to for encouragement and advice? Who can help this disconnected generation if you and I do not? We see many couples in good and even great marriages that tell us that they simply need another couple to act as a sounding board. They need another couple to listen to them, to pray for the things their families would never understand, and to spend time with them. Why do even the best of married couples need another couple in whom to confide? The answer: we treasure the same things—a good marriage and a healthy family. Those who value the same things are more likely to work as a team, as a community, and as a supporting family.

Today the lyrics of the Dean Martin song "Memories are Made of This" may sound unrealistic and a bit corny, but the reality is that this is the plan that God has for most of us. The song journeys through a couple's life together. It starts with the wedding day and moves on to their new home, children being born, the joy that lasts over the years, thanking God for their blessings, and staying married for life. This was the standard years ago. Again, from the outside this may seem like a fanciful wish for dreamy lovers, but truly, from the inside, Dean Martin's song puts into words what most men and women naturally hope for in their lives together. It is because of our scarred hearts that these classic lyrics, which describe the natural and original plan for life and love, seem like a pipe dream to many couples. It doesn't mean that it doesn't take work to have a fruitful and flourishing marriage. When we lose the strength and resolve to work towards the best marriages possible, for ourselves or those we know, then we have failed our God, our spouse, and our family. Let us together work to restore the original plan for marriage, a future full of hope with a God who can make "all things new" (Rev 21:5)!

Mentoring the Cohabiting Couple

Despite our deepest natural longings, we find that most couples have a "rose-colored glasses" view of marriage and a deep fear that marriage will not be any different than cohabitation. Let us explain this seemingly contradictory comment. Most couples are sexually active before marriage—studies show the number to be over 90 percent[2]—and sex results in bonding. Bonding, rose-colored glasses, and seeing your partner through a forgiving lens is wonderful and absolutely necessary AFTER marriage. Prior to marriage these can obscure reality and set a couple up for failure if someone does not guide them in this area. If we are seeing our betrothed through an unrealistic lens, then we are setting him or her up later for an inevitable tumble off the pedestal. We all fall off the pedestal at some point, but hopefully we do not fall too far. When we do fall, we hope our spouse is still willing to catch us or at least pick us up! It is a challenge to explain to couples that the "rose-colored glasses syndrome" is normal part of marriage; however, in engagement, it is a set up for future heartbreak. Most of the couples with whom we discuss this do "get it," and they agree with us. Firm resolution to save sex for marriage and to work on other forms of intimacy often follows this discussion, but not always. We share with them that aside from all the moral reasons they may have heard (although most of them have not even heard these!), there are important psychological reasons for waiting and working on the other forms of intimacy first.

Mentors can help to explain the other forms of intimacy and how they themselves developed these forms of intimacy in their own relationship. Other forms of intimacy are: spiritual (praying together), intellectual (conversations, reading a book or taking a class together), emotional (sharing things deeply with each other without fear of judgment), and physical but not sexual (comfortable displays of affection without them being considered sexual advances). These forms of intimacy are crucial for every married couple and are often lacking or diminished in the relationships of cohabitating engaged couples.

The Fears of a Cohabitating Engaged Couple

This leads us to the deep-seated fear that many cohabiting engaged couples share with us. They often "slide" into marriage and gradually assume the life of a married couple without actually being married. They have lived with each other for years. They share pets, checking accounts, children, bills, and a bed. In their minds, the only thing missing is the wedding ring and some sort of permanence. By the grace of God (usually through a badgering parent or grandparent), they decided to get married in the church. They want to know and they ask us often, "How will marriage be different from just living together as a "committed couple" as we do now? Will we be disappointed? Is marriage going to help us to have a better relationship?" They are serious. So are we.

Mentoring a cohabitating engaged couple is an open invitation to share God's plan for married love with them, and to invite them to save sex for marriage. Why? Because they realize that something is missing in their relationship and that there must be something more. Recently we asked a couple (longtime cohabitors and engaged to be married) what they thought would be different once they were married, presuming they might be able to name a few things. They immediately responded in a very sobering way. They described their number one concern: they could not afford a honeymoon due to expenses from the upcoming wedding and graduate school. In addition, things were tight with their school schedule, and they were not even taking time off from work after the wedding. Interestingly then, the question was turned on us from the couple who asked: "What could be different?" They were looking forward to their wedding day but they were fearful that life would be just the same the day after their wedding.

We who work with engaged couples need to be aware of the fears and hopes that cohabitating couples carry in their hearts as they prepare for marriage. We need to invite them to share their concerns with us and we should gently guide them to consider God's original plan for their relationship and for their marriage. Many of these couples have been living together for years and had been sexually active prior to living together as well. To most people (and even perhaps to themselves), they look like any married couple, with the exception of the missing wedding ring and a shared last name. They felt that moving in together was the big leap to a lifelong commitment, and the wedding was more of a formality. Still, what was evident was a desire for more! Deep down they knew and communicated in subtle ways that something was missing from the relationship they shared. They could not put their finger on what that "something" was and expected us to name and help identify what was missing. Again, this is a great opportunity to evangelize and present the good news about marriage and sexuality.

Oftentimes, we explain to couples in this situation that there are many things that could be different after the wedding, but that the wedding itself does not magically guarantee that things will be different. In all honesty, discovering and living the difference greatly depends on them opening up and allowing things to become different by actively pursuing something different. We ultimately explain that it is not just "something" that would be different but Someone that would begin to be different in a good way! That missing something is actually a "Someone," the Creator of marriage. He wants to give them something that they do not yet possess, but could, if they open themselves up to God's plan for their life together. Here is the invitation for them to see and acknowledge the gift of a sacramental marriage, to want that gift, and to live the gift the best way that they possibly can.

What's the BIG Difference between Cohabiting and Marriage?

Before you read this section ask yourself: "Did we slide into marriage? Do we fit the description of a couple who never made a conscious decision to commit to a life together and enter intentionally into a covenant of marriage? Have we invited God into our relationship to fully and freely live out our wedding vows in Him?" If you are pondering these questions and you begin finding answers to these questions for yourselves, then we can tell you that you are going to be an amazing resource to the young couples who don't know that this is an important question to ask. It will be important for you to have a simple, but often difficult, conversation with cohabiting couples.

If you can have this simple conversation with a couple who is "sliding" into marriage, then you are addressing their very real concerns and opening them up to all that God wants for them. Marriage is not magic. God does not force His grace on us if we do not want it. There has to be a concrete decision to accept the gift of the sacrament of marriage in order for it to change us from the inside out. Without a moment of acknowledging God as the Author of marriage, the couple who slid into marriage may experience a void in their relationship. Marriage ends up becoming another thing "to do" on their bucket list for life. The fundamental difference between living together and accepting the gift of marriage is the difference between a contract and a covenant—a life without grace or a life full of grace.

In addition to describing the graces that marriage has to offer, we need to also explain that the only way that things can be different in their day-to-day life is if they acknowledge the difference between sliding into a relationship and committing to a life-long relationship. This conversation is not an easy one, but it is essential to help form and prepare young couples to open themselves to the graces that will come as they begin to prepare for the sacrament of marriage. These graces help to shed light on the wonderful differences that they will experience in living out the sacrament of marriage. Here

———◇———

Marriage is not magic. God does not force His grace on us if we do not want it. There has to be a concrete decision to accept the gift of the sacrament of marriage in order for it to change us from the inside out.

———◇———

are some topics to discuss with a couple who is sliding into marriage:

◇ The difference between being engaged and being married.
◇ The difference between living together and creating a home and a family together.
◇ The difference between having sex together and having a sacrament together.
◇ The difference between waking up next to someone with whom you share a bed, and waking up next to a spouse to whom your obligation is to be Christ, to witness His Love, and to help get him or her to Heaven.
◇ The difference between just surviving or enduring life and actually celebrating, creating, and giving life.

This begs the question: How can couples authentically live their lives when they are not fully and irrevocably committed to the person with whom they are giving themselves to sexually? This question can cause some angst and distress in your conversation. If they say, "Well, we are totally committed to each other so nothing is going to change after the wedding," then they are probably not being honest with themselves. We must insist that there is a difference, but it depends ultimately on their cooperation and openness to God's plan for their future.

The difference between a cohabiting relationship and a sacramental marriage is huge. The differences are legal, spiritual, practical, and cultural. Once a couple admits that there is a difference, they can then discuss the new way they will give themselves to each other. They can explore together how to invite God into their relationship and how to be open to His plan for their lives. It is at this point in the difficult conversation where we strongly suggest for them to abstain or even separate for the weeks or months before the wedding. Even civilly married couples often decide to abstain in order to fully commit to a covenant of marriage before receiving the sacrament of marriage. This covenant includes God *and* His plan for marriage. Most of the couples with whom we share this do agree to abstain and tell us after the fact that it made all the difference. One couple told us that it was the best decision they had made for their relationship because it kept them from bringing into their sacramental marriage some of the selfishness and insecurity they had experienced when they were cohabiting. In the end, we always say: "Look, you have everything to gain and nothing to lose. Just do it!" No one has ever come back and told us, "Hey, it wasn't worth it." Each of the couples we have challenged to abstain has always returned rejoicing. There is a huge difference between gradually "sliding into marriage"[3] versus committing to marriage. It is the difference between tolerating God or embracing His plan for their future full of hope; enduring marriage preparation or demanding all that it can offer; isolating themselves from friends or mentors or opening themselves up to the beautiful blessings that come from a life lived in solidarity with others.

You must be a witness to all that God has created marriage to be, and you must share that love with others. You must inspire and gently nudge those couples whom God puts in your path. We have been created in the image of God, and marriage is a reflection of the very life of the Trinity. This is the first step, on your part, to restore the luster to the sacrament of marriage and to share your marriage with others. It won't happen overnight but that is no reason not to start today by inviting God to renew your marriage. He will always say, "Yes." Why? Because he is a Father who loves you and wants the best for His children. He wants to use you as reminder to the world of the infinite love that He has for each of us.

Chapter 5

Saying "I Do Each Day: The "Heart" of Our Marriage

In this chapter we would like to reveal the "heart" of our marriage with you and the ways that God has touched our marriage. The following are stories that our friends all know and that we often share with couples at retreats or as a part of marriage preparation classes. Just imagine that you are at our house, staying up late with us, and chatting over a glass of wine. While we may never meet you on this side of Heaven, we hope that this deeply personal chapter will touch your marriage, your ministry, or your relationship with God. These are the stories where God has reached out and touched our lives directly, through circumstances, or indirectly through the witness of other married couples. We share them for your encouragement and pray that they are a blessing to you.

First, we will reveal some things that we found were key to living out our wedding vows long after our wedding day, and then we will share a few stories about the heart of our marriage. We will disclose those "God moments" that remind us that no matter how hard things get, He is tenderly watching over us, and He has plans for a "future full of hope" (Jer. 29:11).

Preparing to Share Your Story with Engaged Couples

As you read this chapter, be thinking about what you would desire to communicate to a young couple if you were to witness through your personal story. Points to consider and discuss with your spouse are:

- ◇ What were some of the things we learned early on in marriage that were a challenge or a surprise, and how did we deal with them?
- ◇ Are we still dealing with them, and are we dealing with them differently now?
- ◇ What is our love story and how is God a part of our story?
- ◇ Do we love each other more now than we did on our wedding day? In what ways?
- ◇ If we could sit with an engaged couple and tell them the most important thing about having a great marriage, what would we say?
- ◇ What do we wish someone had shared with us prior to our wedding and would we have been open to hearing these words of wisdom?
- ◇ What do we think mentoring is all about, and are we already mentoring someone in some way?
- ◇ Do we have a mentor in our lives and in our marriage?

◇ What role does God have right now in our lives?

Learning to Live out our Wedding Vows

St. John of the Cross wisely wrote, "On the evenings of our lives we will be judged on our love."[1] Let's talk about this in reference to our spouses. This does not mean that we must have the "warm fuzzies" every day for our spouse nor does it mean that we must have the honeymoon glow while we struggle to love selflessly. It does mean that when we get up every day, we have to make choices that will bring us closer to our spouse. It means putting God first, and praying as a couple that He will teach our hearts to love like His heart. We do this each day over and over and over again.

When we get up every day, we have to make choices that will bring us closer to our spouse. It means putting God first, and praying as a couple that He will teach our hearts to love like His heart. We do this each day over and over and over again.

What does this decision to love look like? Has there ever been a time when you were just not feeling it? Perhaps you felt like you needed to get away or felt disconnected from your spouse. Perhaps you even felt angry or irritated with him or her, but then you made a very conscious decision to love. You made the decision to do the right thing, to keep living out your wedding vows to honor and respect, and yes, even cherish the other when he or she was getting on your nerves! It was hard, but you knew it was the right thing to do and the right way to love. The decision to cherish rather than wallow in your anger or resentment towards your spouse will be blessed. Perhaps not immediately, but over that day or week, you made that decision again and again to love. We are all human so maybe you slipped up and went back to your anger and resentment. It is hard to love and keep those wedding vows to honor and respect your spouse, but life is much more beautiful when you try over and over again to love, honor, and cherish your spouse.

When we "intentionally mentor" couples, it is with the purpose of sharing our struggles as we try to live out our wedding vows. We have not perfected this area of our marriage, and perhaps it will not be until our deathbed that we finally know how well we lived out our vows, but that should not keep us from sharing our struggles and successes. The point is to make the connection with couples that they should be considering their wedding vows on a *daily* basis and thinking about their decisions in life with reference to their wedding vows.

The Heart of Our Marriage

What is the "heart" of our marriage? If asked, we would both say that it is the desire to consciously live out our wedding vows every day. We live them out each day as if it was our first, last, and only day of our married lives.

This story illustrates the importance of taking seriously the idea of living out our vows. We were married the Saturday after Easter, the eve of Divine Mercy Sunday. We had decided that throughout the Lenten season we would go to the 6:30 a.m. daily Mass at the local Carmelite Monastery.

We were preparing for our life together and asking God to bless our future marriage. Yes, we were a little crazy to be up that early, but we really felt called to do this. There is a good chance that God calls each of us to do some difficult things. Both of us were busy with our work, planning wedding details, and overseeing the building of our house. These early hours of the morning seemed to be the only time of the day that we would see one another. I (Mary-Rose) was living in a small, old, picturesque, three-room "shotgun" style house. For those non-Southern readers, a shotgun house is a small cottage built in a way to be able to cool the house down in the days before air conditioning. These houses have long hallways that catch the breeze, and are called "shotgun" houses because one could stand at the front door and theoretically shoot a gun through the house and out the back door. The landlord was a friend and had fully furnished it with beautiful antiques.

In the winter and early spring the house was cold and drafty, but it had a cozy charm. There was no oven, so I made biscuits from scratch every morning in a toaster oven and brewed a pot of "Community Coffee" (strong Cajun coffee). Every morning I so looked forward to my good morning kiss from Ryan. We had dated long distance for so long that just getting to see Ryan every day was a blessing. We would eat breakfast, pray morning prayer together out of the breviary (a prayer book consisting mostly of readings from scripture and a daily reflection), and then go to Mass at the Carmelite community.

The monastery oozed holiness from its brick walls to the statues and paintings that adorned it. On the wall behind the main altar was a painted scene from Calvary with a quote from St. John of the Cross: "Love is repaid by Love alone." This quote became a large part of our lives and our marriage. It is not so much that that we love because we feel like loving, but because we made a vow to each other before God. We will not be judged by God on our feelings, but rather on our decision to love or not to love! To give in to half-hearted love or selfishness or to give up altogether are not options compatible with living out our promise. If we love as Christ loves, then he repays us with Himself and with His loving heart. Looking back, we treasure those mornings so much! We also see what a source of strength they became for our marriage even before it started.

> "Love is repaid by Love alone." This quote became a large part of our lives and our marriage. It is not so much that that we love because we feel like loving, but because we made a vow to each other before God.

Even now, when we drink coffee and say our morning prayers together (hoping the whole time that our little ones don't wake up!), we still remember those mornings and our deepened resolution to always make time for God in our marriage. Yes, there are days that we do not feel like getting up early, praying, cleaning up messes, or being nice to one another. However, putting God at the center of our marriage makes it just a little easier to remember to honor our wedding vows when we feel like just getting by. There is so much more to marriage than just getting by! As Ryan often says, "Life is meant to be lived not just endured!" These are the kinds of things we share as we mentor couples. We share this heart of our marriage, not because we have perfected living out our wedding vows, but because we honestly want others to experience the same joy of living out the vocation to love! It is so much easier to live out your wedding vows when you are connected with other couples who understand and support you. You can talk about it, mentor one another, and hold each other accountable.

God's Lavish Love

God has been and continues to be an intimate friend and guide in our marriage and family life. He is not just the Author of marriage, but also the Author of life. In this world where embryos are "created" in a petri dish, frozen, selectively reduced and commodified, we often forget that children are a gift from God. Everything about having a family, starting a family and being a family should involve listening to His plan for you. We teach Fertility Awareness (Natural Family Planning) and have seen the hand of God work so intimately in our lives and in the lives of those we teach.

One couple we worked with had been trying for more than five years to get pregnant and had spent a year's salary on In Vitro Fertilization (IVF) with no success. On their final attempt of IVF, the wife contracted the flu and was told that this month she would not be able to come in for the IVF procedure. They discerned that God was the one who was really in charge and committed their future family to God. If He wanted them to have a child, He could give them a child. If they did not get pregnant, they were open to adoption. For the first time, they felt the peace and freedom that comes when you put in God's hands what belongs to Him in the first place. In less than a month they found out they were expecting. You can guess the conception date. Yes, the very same day they had put their family in God's hands. At the time, they were civilly married and God's lavish display of grace in their lives inspired them to return to church. They later had their marriage convalidated and received the sacrament of marriage. We have been inspired by their witness.

There are no Coincidences with God

Before we were even married, we discussed the name we would choose for our first child. We chose the name Zélie which was St. Thérèse of Liseaux's mother's name. St. Thérèse's father, Louis Martin, had wanted to become a priest and her mother, Zélie, had wanted to become a nun. Instead, both felt God was calling them to marriage. Our story was very similar to theirs, and we discovered that we both loved the name Zélie. We decided if our first child was a girl, we would name her Zélie. One month before she was due to arrive, our first child was born via emergency caesarian at 12:03 a.m. on December 23rd. The day Zélie was born could have easily been a tragic day for our family. But after a week in the neo-natal intensive care unit (NICU), we all went home thanking God for the gift of this new little life. A few months later, a dear priest friend brought back some cards from France with photos of Louis and Zélie Martin on them. The cards also listed, in French, the important dates in their lives: their birthdays, wedding date, and dates of death. Zélie Martin had been born on December 23rd, 1831. Truly, there are no coincidences with God!

We were powerfully reminded that God is in control and cares tenderly for us. We knew that the timing of our daughter's birth, her name, her health, and the gift of her life were all very personal gifts from God. It was evidence that God really knows the number of hairs on our heads. More importantly, He knows exactly what our family needs, and He wants to give it to us. It is crucial for you to involve God in the discernment of your family planning. If you are not involving God in this area of your life, then what area of your life does God have access to? Is He invited just when there is an emergency or a need? We have found that God permeates our lives with His blessings, grace, and many tangible traces of his love every day. God loves us perfectly, and we try to love Him even if it is imperfectly. He wants us to live life "fully alive" and full of his love. Living out our wedding vows is how we can visibly love Him back. We can easily substitute the word "spouse" for the word "brother" in the often quoted Bible verse, "for the one who does not love his brother whom he has seen, cannot love God whom he has not seen."[2] To paraphrase, "If you do not love the spouse that you can see, even when you do not feel like it, then how can you love the God that you cannot see?"

Saying "I Do" Each Day

Daily, we try to fully embrace the joys and the challenges (and yes, the sufferings) that are required of all those who are committed to living in a covenant of sacramental matrimony. The big decision we made on our wedding day helps to make the little decisions doable. The big "yes" helps to define and create the environment that enables us to respond to all the necessary "little yesses." Those "little yesses" must take place for a couple who wants to be united and of service to each other. Simply put, we make the choice each day to live our marriage in an intentional way and to keep our wedding day promise to each other.

Even though Ryan and I both have extensive backgrounds in ministry and faith formation, we do not take for granted the effort that is needed to develop good life skills. Being a "religious or spiritual" person does not give you an easy road to a perfect marriage! We all have to learn to love and to deal with each other and our own inadequacies. Only through a love that puts the other first does the daily grind become Heaven on earth—the "one blessing not washed away in the flood.[3]" Every year on our wedding anniversary we repeat our wedding vows to one another, and we re-read the Scripture passages proclaimed at our wedding. Every year, those words mean so much more than they first did on our wedding day. Why? Because on our wedding day, we knew only in theory what we would learn in the years to come. We learned what those vows would look like practically and realistically in everyday life—and that is okay! For example, "to cherish" means to savor and delight in one's spouse. It even means to deal lovingly with the annoying habits which eventually can become endearing, if they don't drive us crazy first. "To honor" means to respect and defend your spouse, even when your girlfriends are "husband bashing," or your buddies are "wife whining." "To love" means that you get up every day and put your spouse first. That is what love is. This is how God loves us. God does not get up every day thinking about Himself, and neither should we.

The heart of our marriage is the commitment to live out our wedding vows every day of our lives. Each day we are called to be more loveable and more loving. Why? So that at the end of our lives we will hear together, "Well done, good and faithful servants. Enter the joy of your Father." Recall the words, of St. John of the Cross: "Love is repaid by Love alone." We pray each day that our life together becomes a beautiful song in which our Heavenly Father rejoices. We ask that our lives remind Him of His original plan for men and women and that our marriage will point others to God and to His perfect love for them.

> Only through a love that puts the other first does the daily grind become Heaven on earth— the "one blessing not washed away in the flood."

Chapter 6

Inside A Mentor Couple's Heart: The Agony & the Ecstasy of Marriage

We have shared just a few things that are at the heart of our marriage. Hopefully, we have stirred in your own heart a desire to recognize what you might be able to offer to couples with whom God has invited you to walk. At this point, we will begin to delve into the history of mentoring, and how we develop a posture that assists you in discerning your response to this call. The specific goal of this chapter is to understand and articulate more effectively all that is true, good, and beautiful about your own participation in the sacramental graces of matrimony.

The Master Artist

Let us begin by acknowledging that today the word "mentor" has definitely been watered down, undervalued, and misunderstood by many. You may be a teacher and someone you don't know, who may not be helpful to you, can be assigned to you as your mentor. At some point, you may have had a "scary" supervisor at work who was classified as your "mentor." You had no choice in either of these situations. These scenarios do not illustrate mentors in the original sense of the word, and definitely not in the sense that we mean here.

One of the best examples that we can use to describe the kind of mentor that we are endeavoring to become is sort of like a master artist and an apprentice. In the literal sense, the term "master" implies one who teaches rather than one who might be considered by others (or even themselves) as "perfect." In a very intimate way, the master artist becomes over time a mentor to his apprentice. Developing in history, the vocation of the master transformed into a role of teaching his apprentice all that he knew, and all that he did, with regards to whatever trade or skill he enjoyed. This mentorship lasted for years or even for the lifetime of the "master" artist.[1] The standard time of an apprenticeship was seven years. After that time, the apprentice was considered a "master." For example, consider the specific talents of a painter. To begin learning the craft of painting, the apprentice began by completing the seemingly menial task of grinding the pigments and compounds that will later be used to make the colorful paints. Under supervision he was allowed to mix these same compounds with each other into paint, and these in turn would be applied to a wall or statute which could last for centuries. This is a simple, yet beautiful, aspect in the development of the "bigger picture" that is easy to overlook. Next, the apprentice would be allowed to pass the paints up to the master artist. He continued by watching the master paint amazing images on a blank canvas. Eventually, the apprentice learned how to fill in large un-detailed portions of the canvas or ceiling, and might work with some slightly more detailed aspects. Over time, the apprentice would be able to create hands and faces, hair moving in a breeze, the soft lighting on an angel's wing, and could painstakingly paint the intricate details of gathered fabric and graceful fingers. The heart of the master is now on that ceiling or canvas for all to see. Only the apprentice knows how it all came together and what stories lie beneath the masterpiece.

When the apprentice finally learns his mentor's secrets, techniques, and all those intangible things that only can be learned over time, it becomes difficult for the skilled critic to tell the difference between the work of the master and his apprentice. The apprentice is taught how to repair and restore both colossal and minute mistakes; how to deal with challenging canvases like ceilings; and how to handle cracks in the wall and imperfections in the material. The master artist has done his job when the apprentice becomes a master artist in his own right. How would that apprentice ever have become a painter, a master in his own right, if the master artist had not first shown him how? What if the master thought that it was not worth teaching someone, that it was a waste of his time? After all, he could have spent his time painting uninterrupted. The apprentice can now pass on to future generations of artists the training he received from the master. If the master had not made the time to instruct his apprentice, all his skill and knowledge would have been buried with him.

Applying the Mentor Model to Marriage

Now let us consider this example in light of what we hope to create between marriage mentors and the young couples whom we have the opportunity to prepare for the biggest decision of their lives. While we have shared the challenging state of marriage, there is another difficult issue to face when mentoring a couple. Our culture can often place marriage on a pedestal. For many the "perfect" image of marriage creates a dissonance for couples who feel that this ideal is impossible for them. So they don't even try! The challenge lies in the limited viewpoint that couples use to see—they only perceive the masterpiece. Unfortunately, the divorce rate numbers can affirm the couples feeling of unworthiness and their own ignorance about the depth of marriage. In our initial conversations with engaged couples we see the great distance between their cultural understanding of marriage and the ideal of marriage taught by their faith community. The ideal seems lovely when walking down the aisle, but not necessarily attainable or sustainable for a lifetime. Many want to progress from enduring an ordinary experience of marriage to embracing the ideal of marriage, but this developmental path is not laid out for them. They take an initial look at themselves and seem to feel that the love they have for each other is embarrassingly insufficient. The prospect of living like this "until death do us part" does not fill them with motivation. Their good feelings come and go, and most couples we talk with understand that. It is important to note and remind those we mentor that love is not necessarily always experienced as an emotion; it has other powerful and more meaningful forms than just emotions. Thank God!

So, how do we uphold and defend the irrevocable beauty of the sacrament of marriage? And, how do we provide for the need to support couples who are trying to live out this awe-inspiring sacrament in the midst of their daily grind? Obviously, this is a huge challenge. However, if you are reading this book, you must be willing to take on the challenge. We cannot simply say, "The church should do something about it," and then wait for it to happen. We are the Body of Christ. We should and can do something about it.

The average couple who may be disillusioned with their relationship is not necessarily a couple who is in a bad or troubled marriage. These are couples who may have a functioning marriage or even a good marriage. Many couples rarely, if ever, have had the opportunity to reflect on what a sacramental marriage truly means. They have never witnessed or experienced the expressions of God's intimate plan for marriage. They have not witnessed the special way He is present to couples who seek to serve each other freely, totally, faithfully, and fruitfully. So, when they begin to understand the beauty of God's plan for marriage, they discover a very personal way of intentionally living their marriage as a vocation. It is our challenge to introduce couples to the beauty of marriage and to continue to walk with them so that they come to fully understand and appreciate God's plan for *their* marriages!

Returning to the master artist analogy, couples need other couples to teach them how to work within the cracks in the wall and fix the discolorations in their relationships.

It helps to have the advice and insights of another couple who has learned how to mix the paints and how to bring all the colors together to make the marvelous masterpiece of married love. In a similar way, this is where the couple who is invited and interested in sharing their marriage begins to share the working plan behind the "masterpiece" of their own married lives.

The Agony & the Ecstasy of Marriage

All marriages should be a masterpiece in progress. You may have wondered if you will ever be finished working on your marriage. There is often an anxiety in knowing that you are working on an important project and just want it to be finished. We are completing our masterpiece of marriage stroke by stroke, through daily self-denials such as the times we go out of our way to show our spouse how much we love him or her, in the ways we work on those deep dark places in our lives, and by the manner that we bring laughter and joy to our daily challenges.

There is a great scene in the film *The Agony and the Ecstasy* where Michelangelo is painting the ceiling of the Sistine Chapel. It is tedious work that takes the artistic genius a very long time to complete. Exasperated, Pope Julius finally comes into the chapel and in agony yells at Michelangelo, "When will my ceiling ever be finished!" In our marriages we are often either Michelangelo or Pope Julius. We are either working hard on the tiny, laborious details of our marriage, or we are standing back and trying to look at the big picture and in desperation yelling (sometimes at our spouse), "Will this marriage ever be perfect? Will I ever be perfect? Will my spouse ever be perfect?" The answer to all of these is a resounding "No."

Potential mentor couples should reflect on the way they have journeyed together as a couple and ponder the sacrifice, patience, and commitment required to continue on the journey. Mentors will begin to see how they helped to form the untutored apprentice couple into one who desires to become a master artist and a mentor to others seeking to live out a sacramental marriage.

You may be thinking, "There is no way that we are the ones to show another couple the path to the masterpiece of marriage." We frequently think the same thing ourselves. We all encounter couples who have totally different lifestyles, interests, or political views. For example, we have worked with engaged couples who had worked in fast food restaurants, waste management, hospitals, or in the oil and gas fields. Of these people, some are introverts and shy barely saying a word, and others are extroverts giving you little opportunity to get a word in edgewise. It seems that, regularly, there is a need for us to overcome our own insecurities and begin to

—————◇—————

> Mentors will begin to see how they helped to form the untutored apprentice couple into one who desires to become a master artist and a mentor to others seeking to live out a sacramental marriage.

—————◇—————

exercise the gifts and graces given to each of us called into ministry. Our question to you is: "Who told the great artists that they were great?"

All artists from the beginning of their practice are not perfect. We study many of their novelties, their mistakes, and eccentricities in art class. In reality, it was their imperfections that shaped their skills, allowing for their art to stand the test of time. Similarly, there is no magic formula to become the "perfect" married couple. There should be no excuse for any of us to wait to share our marriage. If there are areas in your own marriage that you believe need some work, then see this as a great opportunity to get started!

How often do you hear from friends and family the tragedy of a couple crushed under the seemingly inevitable decision of a divorce? You really want to help but you have nothing to say. You want to do something, but there's nothing you can do that would seem helpful. This is the experience of those who watch good friends or family members suffer needlessly. This is also a common challenge of well-intentioned people of faith trying to speak to an individual's difficult circumstances in a secular culture that promotes tolerance and individual happiness above what is best for a family or community. We do a good job of convincing ourselves that we do not know the struggling couple well enough to talk to them. Yet, we wonder what might have happened if there had been a couple who had befriended them and guided them and developed a relationship of trust and support? We know that the habits of isolation, selfishness, and individual preoccupations that predispose others for divorce, can be addressed effectively by couples who have overcome these regularly-occurring obstacles in any relationship. Be that kind of couple for another couple!

Church-based Mentoring

If your church does not have a mentor-based marriage preparation ministry, please speak with your pastor and recommend that one be started. A better approach than using church-appointed mentors is creating the opportunity for couples to choose their own mentors. We have found this out in our own ministry through the "Witness to Love" program. Regardless of whether the couple you mentor has chosen you or whether the church assigned them to you, the way that you will prepare to share your marriage with them is usually the same. We are not saying that church-appointed mentors should not be used. These trained mentor couples can be a great resource to their communities. What we do suggest is that these mentor couples invite the engaged couples to choose another couple whom they admire to join them at a halfway point in the process. The church-appointed mentors would "pass the baton" to the friends whom the engaged couple has chosen. This ensures that when the engaged couple is married, there will be a couple who is regularly in their lives to witness to them and to support them.

These are the steps that we use in the formation of mentor couples in our parish. They will be unpacked in the next chapter:

1. Reflect with your spouse what you think are the areas of your relationship that have grown the most since you first got married.
2. Try to understand how you worked through those issues and made them a defining strength in your relationship.
3. For those issues that are still occurring, discuss how you are working on them and what you would share that would benefit another couple.
4. Make sure you have a good list of questions or conversation starters for your conversations with them.
5. Build a relationship with the couple that you are mentoring.
6. Share your marriage and accompany the couple you are mentoring.
7. Sustain the friendship and continue as mentors! Do not have this become a short term "hobby" for fixing a couple and then let the friendship slide.
8. Pray for them, and let them know you are praying for them.

By all means, help any couple that you can, but don't minimize the importance of building relationships by sharing the heart of your marriage with others. In the future, when challenging times come, they will have another couple to lean on. Too often those couples who are experiencing challenges in their marriage isolate themselves from help. When we find out that they are separated or divorced, we also find that there was no one close enough who could guide them at the first signs of difficult marital issues. The friends who were worried about them did not have the tools or relationships outside of their marriage to help them. In the end, their hands were tied. They could only prepare themselves for the train-wreck of a marriage coming down the tracks. Commit to begin establishing relationships now with couples who are just getting started. That way, when the challenges come, you will not feel that your only option is to wring your hands as you watch a marriage be torn apart by confusion, selfishness, despair, and anger.

We will have a chapter at the end of this book that will deal specifically with working with those in troubled marriages, but here we simply want to emphasize the importance of forming bonds of connection with other couples to whom you feel God calling you--not superficial and casual interactions, but deep and lasting friendships which are marital lifesaver in the future. Just as we felt drawn to our spouse, there are also other couples that we feel drawn to as "couple friends," and they feel drawn to us. These are couples that God puts in our lives to teach us, and for us to teach them. We all learn from each other, support each other, and grow at different paces. It is not just about worrying about another couple or keeping tabs on them—when you give, you are always receiving much more. We hear comments like, "Reflecting on what our marriage has been was both healing and challenging at the same time. It was also a good reminder that we should never stop where we are, and that we should never tire of trying to do better."

When we encourage mentor couples to share their marriages with engaged couples through the "Witness to Love" ministry at our church, they frequently communicate their surprise at how much their marriage was blessed during this process. The common theme for many of these mentor couples is the more satisfying experience of giving rather than receiving. It is the experience that many of us have of receiving so much more than we give away. Most of us never really go into these new mentoring relationships with the intention of receiving something. (It seems like most of the time we are just trying to work out all of the logistical details and be on time for a meeting!) However, over and over again, the mentors find themselves enriched, more in love with each other and with

> Here we simply want to emphasize the importance of forming bonds of connection with other couples to whom you feel God calling you--not superficial and casual interactions, but deep and lasting friendships which are marital lifesaver in the future.

our Lord, than they may have been before the journey. They are renewed in their commitments to their married family members and on the way they become a real light on a hill in their communities. Why? Because love is "diffusive." True love is Christ-like love compelling us to share that love with others. We all know couples like this—they are a delight to all who know them and it is a joy to be around them! Being around them helps you see the gift of marriage as a treasure. The good news is that you absolutely can be that kind of couple for someone else. Yes, you.

Chapter 7

Mentoring the "Un-Married"

HERE's the next big question: "Who are the "un-married" whom you may be called to mentor, and what do they need from you? Broadly speaking, the unmarried are all those children, teens, college students, young adults, engaged, single, cohabiting, or anyone in the "I am not ready for marriage" category that you know. We will discuss the many opportunities that exist for you to witness to the goodness and permanence of marriage and how you can share the particular gifts of your marriage with the "un-married." You will build upon conversations you can have with those who are considering engagement, cohabiting (engaged or not), or currently engaged. In this chapter you will learn how you and your spouse can penetrate deeply into your relationship and come to understand how you can share your marriage with those preparing for marriage or considering marriage. This chapter is intended to be both practical and instructional. In addition, the steps for preparing to be a great mentor listed in the last chapter will be fleshed out so that you can come away with a potentially new set of skills and better insights into the ones you already have.

An Examination of Marriage

As you prepare to share your marriage with others, please prayerfully consider the following questions for reflection. A thorough, honest and prayerful study of how your marriage can grow is not wasted time. Not only will it strengthen your marriage, but it will also reveal the treasures of your marriage that can help to sustain other couples. Here are some of the general questions that you will want to ask yourselves and the couple you are mentoring. We strongly suggest you discuss the following questions with your spouse *prior* to discussing them with another couple:

◇ Have our personal experiences and decisions set us up to be more likely to struggle, flourish, or even fail in marriage?

◇ How have these issues played out over the years in our relationship before and after marriage?

◇ What causes the key issues to resurface, or are they present on a daily basis?

◇ Did I/we "slide" into marriage, or was it a conscious decision to marry?

◇ What can we do together to combat the divorce and cohabitation statistics?

◇ What issues do we BOTH already struggle with or are currently struggling with?

◇ What are the signs or issues that suggest we need help in our marriage?

◇ What is our plan when we need help?

◇ How long will we wait to get help?

◇ What are some things we would agree are important enough for which to seek help?
◇ Whom will we go to for help?
◇ Even though I am the mentor, do I also have a mentor in my marriage?

Once you have discussed, prayed through, and reviewed the previous questions, ask yourself two additional questions.

◇ What are the "gems," the key takeaways from your discussions on each of these questions?
◇ What is your couple game plan for working on any potential issues in your own marriage?

This list of questions is the beginning of many discussions that *all* couples should have *prior* to marriage, especially those couples who have a higher risk of divorce. This is important. Your conversation should be a series of ongoing discussions and should not be only a one-time event. These questions can be modified for your use with a couple who is struggling to stay married. These are discussions that every married couple should have at some point, even if they have been "comfortably" married for some time. Discussions like these will bear fruit in your relationship. Later when you finish reading this book, you will want to revisit this list with your spouse and gain new insights into the gift, meaning, and purpose of your marriage.

Becoming a Marriage Advocate

Now we would like to present just a quick overview of the historical and current background of marriage preparation.

Why are we not experiencing some better results with these preparation programs? Why is the divorce rate for those getting married in church still between 28 percent and 39[1] percent? How do you know your marriage preparation process is working? This discussion is especially helpful if you are reading this book as a marriage preparation mentor and are not familiar with the marriage preparation process in most churches.

There has been a relentless disintegration of the basic fabric of community. The culture surrounding marriage, family life, community, and their interaction has gradually broken down. The institutions which have always been regarded as advocates for the rearing and education of children by their parents have lost their belief that parents are the primary educators of their children. What we experienced was the sobering reality that you cannot just "educate" a couple for marriage and then send them back into their broken community or family life. The aptly-named "no-fault divorce"[2] law that originated in California in 1969 said that the "dissolution of a marriage does not require a showing of wrongdoing by either party."[3] This means that if a couple is "incompatible," they can simply walk away. What safeguard is there to encourage a couple to work through their incompatibilities? Men and women, by the simple fact that they are men and women, will always have irreconcilable differences. Men and women are irreconcilably different from one another.

Divorce begets divorce, and divorce causes a breakdown in family life. The breakdown of the nurturing family unit in turn causes a breakdown in the connection between extended family and communities. At any family reunion (if you even have them) you find that the commonly understood definition of a family as father and mother and children is not the norm. The original nuclear family that includes father, mother, and children is an endangered species at many of our holiday gatherings. One of the number one fears that engaged couples bring up in our conversations is, "How in the world will we make it to all of our family's scheduled events for Christmas, Thanksgiving, or Easter?" Many are trying to figure out how to include two sets of stepparents, an ex-spouse or two, step siblings, and the grandparents! Holidays become confusing, exhausting and depressing for children. No matter what the contributing factor, the disintegration of the family's place in community is a fact, and it is impacting marriages and families everywhere. The focus is not on how to return to the way it used to be, but to focus on what worked in the past and what works today for creating successful, happy, and lasting marriages. The preparation of engaged couples for marriage and the renewal of existing marriages is the number one way to protect marriages in the future!

> Many are trying to figure out how to include two sets of stepparents, an ex-spouse or two, step siblings, and the grandparents! Holidays become confusing, exhausting and depressing for children.

Safeguarding marriage is the key to fighting poverty, depression, suicide, sexual abuse, crime, and isolation. If you are a "numbers" person, just looking at the cost of divorce for the American taxpayer will stun you. The Institute for American Values did a first-ever study of the total annual cost of divorce and they found that, "... we can be confident that current high rates of family fragmentation cost taxpayers at least $112 billion per year."[4] That is billion, not million! If you needed that extra motivation to do something to help today's couples have happy and lasting marriages, then perhaps this can be your motivation.

Practical Ways to Fight the Divorce Statistics

We will examine how the indicators for divorce can be remedied by using our "Scavenger Hunt" list during the marriage preparation process. How a couple comes to the altar is just as important as how a couple leaves the altar. What do we mean by this? *Time* magazine summed it up very well:

> Every wedding is haunted by that axiom, "Half of all marriages end in divorce." But it's not a random coin flip. At the time of a couple's wedding, there are factors already present that can raise the odds of divorce to as high as 70 percent, or lower it to nearly 20 percent.[5]

You may be wondering what those factors are and how you can help. As we sifted through the many studies on marital success and failure, we found that Randal Olsen had some of most practical studies listed on his website www.randalolsen .com. We have reviewed his and many studies and below you

will find some of the key indicators for marital success that
you can share with the couples you mentor:

- ◇ Couples who cohabitate prior to engagement
  or prior to marriage have a higher chance of
  divorce. Remember we discussed "sliding"
  into marriage versus choosing to be married?
  Couples who slide into marriage have a much
  higher chance of divorce. Making an intentional commitment can tip the scale toward
  marital success.[6]
- ◇ The longer the dating period is before engagement, the better. Those who date at least one to
  two years before their engagement have a much
  higher chance of marital success. So, if the
  couple you are mentoring is considering a short
  dating period with a quick engagement, share
  with them that the research shows that a longer
  period of dating equals a higher marital success
  rate. Dating or courting three or more years
  before getting married leads to the most stable
  marriage.[7]
- ◇ Financial stability is also an indicator of marital
  success. This does not mean that engaged couples need to wait until they have lots of money
  to get married, but it does mean that to stack
  the cards in their favor, they should have financial goals and stability before the wedding.[8]
- ◇ How often a couple goes to church and how
  often they pray together are indicators for

marital success.[9] Couples who never go to
church are two times more likely to divorce
than those who go to church regularly.[10] This
statistic in and of itself should be enough to get
a couple to come to church with you!

◇ An overly concerned attitude about one's
future spouse's appearance is also a red flag
and an indicator for divorce. This is a great
item to discuss with couples. How they
appear to others, especially their appearance
or financial standing, should not be a deep
concern.[11]

◇ How many people attend the wedding is
another indicator for marital success or failure. Obviously those who elope or have very
small weddings have a higher chance of divorce
because they have less support from their family and friends. Encourage them to have a less
costly wedding where they invite more friends
and family.[12]

◇ How much is spent on the wedding is also an
indicator of divorce. The more you spend on
the wedding day, the more likely you are to be
divorced. Remind the couple that the wedding day is one day, but the marriage is for a
lifetime.[13]

◇ If too much money is spent on the wedding it
is possible that the honeymoon is postponed or
doesn't even happen. Strongly discourage your
couple from letting this happen. Even if the

honeymoon means going to a friend's camp or vacation home for a week, encourage this![14]

◇ Coming from a family of origin where one or both parents are divorced is also an indicator for divorce, but it does not have to be! A couple can be committed to never putting their children through what they endured. Recently, we spoke with a newlywed couple who explained that while both of them had come from a divorced home, they had discussed at length that they would do everything possible to ensure that their children never went through the same thing.[15]

◇ If the bride has a poor relationship with her father, it will increase a couple's odds of divorce; this can be partially resolved if she can develop a strong relationship with the groom's father.[16]

◇ Waiting until you're more mature to get married will increase your chances of marital stability. Those who get married young have a higher chance of a divorce than those who are more mature and settled when they marry. If you're working with a young couple, help them to discern whether getting married sooner or later is better. This is especially important today because of the high cost of education.[17] This leads us to the next factor.

◇ Those who have more education are more likely to have stable marriages. This is partly because it adds to the financial stability, maturity, and increased age of the partners at the time of their marriage.[18]

◇ Those who are kind to their future spouse will have a much higher chance of marital success and happiness. This sounds simplistic but for those of us who have been married for more than five years, you might realize the significance of this factor.[19]

◇ One of the most important indicators is this: Does the potential groom help his future bride with basic tasks, or does he sit around while she serves a meal? This is something that we see again and again with couples. Older couples like to point this out to younger couples. They will say in front of the young engaged couple, "Hey, watch out, boy! You had better open that door for your fiancée," or, "Girl, you know if he won't help you with the dishes now, he will never change a diaper." How regularly a man is willing to help his fiancée with tasks that are not necessarily "his tasks" is an indicator of marital success.[20] It is important for you to share this information with couples and even cite studies if necessary. This is a great opportunity to share how you may have grown as a couple in this area. Just do it with some humor. If it seems more prudent, take them aside and discuss it individually before you bring it up together when you share as couples.

Getting Involved in the Marriage Preparation Process

In addition to understanding the indicators for marital success, you will also want to know what is involved in the marriage preparation process. As a mentor you will want to know how you will directly or indirectly participate in this process. Depending on where a couple is in proximity to their wedding day, there may be different ways that you help them to understand and live out the sacrament of marriage. Throughout the marriage preparation process, there are those who contribute to a couple's preparation remotely and immediately.

Remote preparation is the preparation that they receive by observing other couples and their parents. This includes Sunday school classes, youth group meetings or retreats. Remote formation is done primarily within the context of a relationship. Consequently, the preparation has far more impact, for better or for worse, on the individual's understanding of marriage. Think about it. Remote preparation is happening all the time in the way friends' parents talk to each other, in the way they see their older siblings or cousins interacting with boyfriends or girlfriends, and in the way they observe the marriages all around them.

In an article written for "Public Discourse" a young lady describes how she drew her conclusions about marriage from observing the intimate relationships of those in her community. She notes that:

> When a couple arrives at engagement, they necessarily bring with them a set of ideas and

experiences about intimacy in relationships that shapes their understanding of, and expectations for, married life. My own understanding of marriage was deeply rooted in the conclusions I drew from observing the intimate relationships modeled in my community, as well as from a more formal engagement, with the ideas communicated to me from family, friends, mentors, and teachers.[21]

Have you ever thought about the impact that correcting your husband when he places the wrong cut of meat in your grocery cart has on the future marriage of the store cashier who is checking your groceries? Did you ever think that the way you opened the car door for your wife could impact a young woman's choice of her future husband? Have you ever thought of how any seemingly small action could impact the future discernment and marriages of those who observed you?

Consider the formation that your "unintended" actions can have on someone who has no deep involvement in your life and is simply observing your behavior. Now consider how much *more* your intentional actions can change the lives of the young couples whom you do know. Offer to take them out for coffee. Invite them into your home. Share your marriage and family life with them. Give them a glimpse of what married life is all about. These interactions will give them a desire for what is real, a desire for something more.

Next there is the other more "immediate preparation," as it is called. Most likely this is the step of preparation in which you would be assisting a couple as you mentor them.

Examples include: the premarital inventory (a list of questions about important items to discuss prior to marriage), meetings with a priest, pastor, or deacon, and attending any conference or retreat that is required. As you can see, the majority of the preparation considered formal preparation happens very close to the wedding date. Sadly, this preparation does not usually focus on welcoming the engaged couple into a community or church. It is simply information, and unfortunately no lasting connection is made with the engaged couple.

Connecting Couples to their Church Community

Marriage preparation should integrate, welcome, and receive the engaged couple into their faith community and into the life of the Church. This is key! Couples willing to share their marriage and accompany engaged couples after the wedding are the ones who will heal the broken sense of community, renew the marriage prep process, create deep and lasting friendships, and encourage flourishing family life. Immediate marriage preparation is almost never done within the context of a friendship. This is a missed opportunity in which to build two couples up together, as a guard against the challenges that every newly married couple will face.

We have said that broken marriages lead to broken communities. Here we are trying to reverse the process by building community *and* strengthening marriages. Do you see how the two work together? When couples are isolated, their incompatibilities can seem magnified because they

are not seeing other couples interact. They are not accountable to anyone, and they do not see the fruits of living out
their wedding vows even when the going gets tough. They
are out of touch with reality and out of the reach of those
who could help them. They live in a broken community, and
when their marriage begins to crumble, there is no one to
lean on for help. Strong community life will always mean
stronger marriages.

Why Trust and Relationships are Key to Successful Marriage Preparation

Prior to testing out the novel idea of letting engaged
couples chose their own mentors (as a means of anchoring
them in their community and
giving them future support),
we had some amazing couples
in our parish who had been
trained to mentor any engaged
couples who asked. What we
discovered, for the most part,
was the engaged couples were
just going through the motions
and did not connect to their
assigned mentors. There were
exceptions, but what usually
happened was that the engaged couple was being "forced"
to discuss very personal things with a couple with whom
they had no connection. Even if some progress was made
in specific areas of their relationship, they had no intention

> We have said that broken marriages lead to broken com-munities. Here we are trying to reverse the process by building community *and* strengthening marriages.

of going back to this mentor for help in the future. Once they were married and finished with mentoring, they would not need to experience such an awkward conversation ever again! After the wedding, many of them disappeared from the community only to be seen again for a baptism class for their first child or tragically when others discovered that they had divorced.

They never reached out to their assigned mentors who never knew they were having problems. We did not know the married couple was having problems because they were not integrated into our church community. We were taking someone from a broken community and attempting to have a parishioner whom they didn't know try to minister to them. We needed to find a better way of incorporating and welcoming couples into the life of our community so when challenging times came there would be a stronger connection to the church community. How can you help a couple who never is really connected to your church community? We had failed to serve couples in the way that they most needed to be served. I was reminded of the question that I had asked couples hundreds of times: "Is there someone whose marriage you admire and with whom you would like to spend more time?" This prompted us to take to prayer the possibility that there was a new way of doing things. It seemed like a new way of doing things but, in fact, it was actually the old way of doing things. It was all about building communities and putting the marriage preparation process back in the context of interpersonal relationships.

For many reasons marriage preparation should be done in the context of a relationship. The main reason is that a newly married couple who is struggling should be able to go straight to the couple with whom they originally discussed

> We were taking someone from a broken community and attempting to have a parishioner whom they didn't know try to minister to them. We needed to find a better way of incorporating and welcoming couples into the life of our community so when challenging times came there would be a stronger connection to the church community.

the issue openly during preparation. How much easier is it to turn to a couple friend and say, "Hey, remember when we discussed in marriage preparation that the "warm-fuzzies" would become less common and not an everyday occurrence? I recall that you said it would not mean that my marriage is on the rocks. Well, I feel like it is on the rocks because I just don't feel anything right now. Work is draining, we are tired, and we just don't have the time and energy for each other that we did in the past." Then their mentor could say, "Yes, I remember that conversation, and I have been where you are. Maybe you should consider putting a little bit more energy

into connecting with your spouse, even when you are tired and don't feel the romance like you did when you were first married." Most of us would much rather share our struggles with a trusted friend than with a stranger! Best of all, friends can hold friends accountable in ways that strangers cannot.

Accountability is not only healthy but is also a bonding opportunity. It is one of the most important roles that a mentor couple will play in strengthening a future marriage. We will list some of the key items that mentors, as accountability partners, can use for discussion with engaged couples. Being an accountability partner also means that you are working on all of these areas in your own marriage. We will list topics for discussion and some questions you can have couples discuss prior to the wedding and again after the wedding.

Preparing to live out your vows:

◇ Are you honoring your betrothed in how you talk to and about him/her?

◇ Do you love your future spouse for how they make you feel, how they look, or what they do for you, or do you love them as a gift from God that you need to get to Heaven?

◇ Are you faithful to them or do you fantasize about others?

◇ Do you entertain past romantic relationships?

◇ Do you dabble in pornography or romance novels?

◇ Is there a way in which you do not plan to give your whole self to your future spouse?

◇ Are you freely sharing who you are with your future spouse, or are you trying to be someone you are not?

Finances:
- ◇ Are you careful with your money and/or your future spouse's money?
- ◇ Are you living in a way that is within your means, or are you living in a way that will put a strain on your marriage and your ability to raise a family?
- ◇ Have you made financial goals together and are you working towards them?

Relationship with God:
- ◇ Are you praying together every day as a couple?
- ◇ Have you found a church that you have become connected to?
- ◇ Are you giving back to that church community?
- ◇ Are you committed to raising your children in a relationship with God?

Conflict Resolution:
- ◇ Have you found the best way to discuss challenging issues?
- ◇ Do you know how to take time out or give your partner time to reflect on an issue?
- ◇ Is the culture within your relationship conducive to asking for forgiveness?

In addition to the short list of questions we just gave, there are some other areas that mentors should discuss with engaged couples. These are topics that easily lend themselves to discussion in your own marriage. Some ideas to get you started are:

◇ What are your fears and dreams about marriage?

◇ What are your hopes and dreams for your life together? Are they realistic?

◇ How do you plan to make important decisions as a couple?

◇ What do you consider to be infidelity? Is pornography infidelity?

◇ How committed are you to this being a lifetime marriage?

◇ What are your pet peeves about technology usage? What rules will there be for you and your family regarding the use of cell phones, video games, social media, TV, etc.?

◇ What do you hope will change about your future spouse but know that it most likely won't?

◇ Who are your friends? Are any of them a challenge to your relationship, i.e., Do they cause conflicts between you or make you question your commitment to each other?

◇ How will you handle in-laws and their interaction with your new family unit, especially when it comes to children?

◇ Do you have a budget, and who is going to balance it and pay bills?

◇ Where is your future home going to be? How will you decide?

◇ Have you discussed planning for your retirement?

◇ Have you thought about where to send your kids to school, and how you are going to pay for it, if necessary?

◇ Have you discussed pets?

◇ Are you expecting to go on vacation? What is the goal of a vacation? When, where, how often, with whom, and at what expense?

◇ Are you planning to go on a couple's retreat or some other marriage-strengthening event regularly?

◇ What illnesses run in your families and how do you cope with illness?

◇ How would you cope with or plan for job loss?

◇ Have you discussed responsible parenthood or considered a mode of family planning that is proven to strengthen marriages? (More on this in the next chapter.)

◇ What is your mode of giving and receiving love? Have you read or discussed "The Five Love Languages: The Secret to Love That Lasts"?[22] (See resources listed at the end of this book.)

◇ What are your holiday or birthday expectations or traditions?

◇ Are you planning on, or even just considering, going back to school for a degree or training? If yes, when and why?

This is not an exhaustive list, but it should at least get you started as you prepare to discuss these questions in reference to your own marriage, and when you share your marriage with another couple. You will want to make sure that any stories you share with them serve their relationship and are not just "stories of your wonderful life." Make sure to decide what the "gem" of each discussion of these topics will be. That is what you will want to share with the engaged couple as you mentor them.

Sending Engaged Couples on a relationship-building "Scavenger Hunt"

Here is a list of some things that we found are excellent ways to encourage a stronger relationship between you and the engaged couple as you mentor them into community life. At our church, we call this list of safeguards against divorce the "Scavenger Hunt." It is to be completed prior to the wedding. These are just some of the items that we encourage couples to do with their mentors. Every couple is different so this is more of a generic list:

◇ Go on a double date with the couple you are mentoring, and do something outdoors. Let the guys plan the date with the ladies in mind. Make it a bonding experience, and do this prior to having any deep discussions.

◇ Set aside times to pray together for your marriage or future marriage.

◇ Go on a weekly date night (both mentor and engaged couple) and hold the other accountable. Watching TV does not count as a date!

- Invite them to go to church with you, or go to church with them a couple of times a month.
- Get to know their family and let them get to know yours.
- Encourage them to go on a couples retreat if they do not already need to go as a requirement.
- Meet with them and their pastor after their retreat, if possible. Have them share with you what they learned and encourage them to ask you any questions they might have.
- Invite them to attend an event at your church.
- Suggest that they find a couple married 50 years or more. Have them ask the couple what their "secret" is and to share their secret with them.
- Invite them to get together with you at least once a month before the wedding to discuss some of the items we listed earlier in this chapter.
- Read a good book with them and discuss.
- Introduce them to another couple whom you admire.
- Help them to make couple friends who are living out their wedding vows and are also recently married.

In the days and weeks leading up to the wedding you will want to avoid "staying out of their hair." Rather, continue to support them and let them know that you will be there for them after the wedding. The common tendency is to give couples their space as the wedding approaches and leave them alone after the wedding. If you are really supporting them, helping them, praying for them, and being a witness to them, then why in the world would your absence be doing them a favor?

As you look back over the time that you have spent helping them to prepare for a life together—a decision that will affect them until "death do us part"—remember that it is not an encounter or a mission that is now over. It is just the beginning! You should be able to see a tangible change in their relationship and in yours. Take some time with them to identify what those tangible changes are. Perhaps, even discuss those areas in which they still need growth. Assure them that you will continue to be present in their lives to offer support, friendship, and guidance. If you have received something that enriched your marriage by observing them in their relationship, let them know. That will be a great encouragement to them, especially when they go through a difficult time.

If they sought you out to be their mentors, then it would be worthwhile to ask them why they chose you. You may be surprised at their response. If you are the ones who offered to mentor them, let them know why you saw something special in their relationship, and share why you want to continue to be involved in their lives. In today's culture, these soul-touching conversations often seem awkward and out of place, but it is only through conversations like these that we can touch and change the hearts of others.

What does a "Diffusive" or "Shared" Marriage Look Like?

What about your own marriage? Is it diffusive? How does it positively impact others? What does a "diffusive" or "shared" marriage look like? It was said in the early Church that Christians knew each other by their love for one another. Do our friends and family know we are Christians by our love for our spouse? We are called to be witnesses to the love in the heart of Christ for each of us. What better way to witness that love than by loving our Divine Spouse—Jesus--and not being ashamed to let others see our love for Him! It is not a matter of a few hours of work but rather it is a "life's work." Have you ever been at a funeral for the spouse of someone who was happily married for 50, 60, or 70 years? There is no more fitting testimony to love than the witness of decades of selfless love. In the funeral parlor you may hear the grandchildren saying how they can't even comprehend loving someone for that long! Teens might have a new "significant other" every semester or more! Yet, here they are seeing with their eyes and their hearts what "'til death do us part" really looks like. That means that only death—not sickness, heartache, boredom, an affair, a challenging personality— can separate them. They meant it.

Recently, we were at the funeral for a friend of ours who had been married for over 60 years. This couple had an extraordinary courtship that would make for a bestselling novel. Greg was in college and took a winter vacation at a ski lodge in a remote mountain town in Canada. While walking the streets of this winter wonderland, he looked up at the balcony of one of the ski lodges and saw a girl. He was instantly attracted to her. He walked inside and asked for her. As it turned out, her father was the owner of the lodge. Leonie and Greg talked all night, and the next day Greg had to drive over 1,000 miles to return to college after his holiday break. He promised Leonie to return every weekend. At that time there was no airport, and the interstate system as we know it had not been built yet. The minute his class ended that next Friday, Greg drove 1,000 miles, on snowy country roads across the Great Lakes area and remote parts of Canada, to keep his promise to Leonie. He made it there just to spend a few hours talking to her before he would have to drive all the way back for class on Monday. He did this every weekend he could until they were married. His wife retold their love story to us at the funeral reception. Leonie was celebrating their life, their marriage, their love. She was glowing. When we left, we felt that we had been at a wedding rather than a funeral. We recalled the love, respect, and humor that anyone in their presence could not help but witness. Even if you did not know the story of their courtship, you would know that this couple had an extraordinary relationship, and they loved to share it with others.

Here's the goal: continue to look for ways that your marriage can be diffusive. If your marriage is not diffusive, by not sharing from your deepest treasure, then you are not fully living out your marriage as it was designed to be lived. Share your marriage and rejoice in it! Your love for each other as spouses should compel you both to share the gift of God's love made manifest in your marriage. The couples you walk with should recognize and desire the infinite love for you from the Father, displayed in your finite love. God's endless love is poured out into those couples who try to live in communion with Him. Others who observe you and your spouse should be inspired to live in relationship with God. This is not a preached love but a lived love.

Chapter 8

After "I Do":
Continuing the Mentorship

THEIR wedding cake top is frozen and preserved for a future wedding anniversary. This future anniversary celebration, depending on the couple's commitment to live out their wedding vows, may or may not happen.

If only preserving a marriage was as easy as preserving a wedding cake! Sadly (or happily), a relationship cannot be preserved on ice and its future thus insured.[1] At some point, either weeks or months after the wedding day, there may come a day when a new bride or new groom will wonder if he or she married the right person. It may come as a surprise, but this is completely natural! Every couple that confides this "shameful" secret to us is surprised to find out that most of us feel that way at some point in our marriage journey. That is why we made wedding vows! We would not need vows if we were divine; but because we are human, we need vows as a way of publicly committing ourselves to remain with *this* person until death.

Tools for Discussion

We share these insights about commitment and the living out of our vows because it is very important that you communicate these truths to the couple you are mentoring, especially after the wedding. This chapter will focus on the ways that you can continue the mentorship you started earlier. There are many new topics you can discuss with them, but without the following tools in place, those discussions may not be as fruitful. These discussion tools can help couples through the tough times by:

⋄ focusing on the value of commitment
⋄ helping them to deepen their relationship with God
⋄ teaching habits that will help increase their chances of marital success
⋄ building community

The Value of Commitment

First, let's discuss the value of commitment. Recently, while on a road trip, we attended Sunday Mass and heard a priest describing the reason for commitment in marriage. We expected him to say all the standard things about couples not getting married today, but instead he went on to describe the dilemma in which many find themselves. They want security but do not want to commit to anything if they don't know what the future holds. The incredible irony of this is that commitment itself is a protection against what the future may or may not hold. The very insecurity that prevents us from making vows keeps us from the security that the vow will provide in the future. This Irish priest's homily reminded us of G.K. Chesterton's famous essay "In Defense of Rash Vows," which aptly describes the dilemma of making a vow and all that it entails. For the rest of the road trip, we continued to discuss the irony of the predicament in which so many couples find themselves. We have quoted the most important lines of this essay below:

> The man who makes a vow makes an appointment with himself at some distant time or place. The danger of it is that himself should not keep the appointment. And in modern times this terror of one's self, of the weakness and mutability of one's self, has perilously increased, and is the real basis of the objection to vows of any kind.[2]

How many times have you heard the phrase, "Love is not a feeling?" This truth is important to remember in your own lives, and it is even more important to remind young couples of it. If love was just a feeling, then on Judgment Day we would be judged on our feelings! We are not going to be judged on our feelings. Rather, we will be judged on how well we lived out our vows. Thank God He doesn't judge us on our feelings. Otherwise, our eternal salvation would depend on that morning cup of coffee, what we ate for lunch, or how we slept last night. God knows better. Love is a decision. That is why we make vows, and that is why we commit for better or for worse. It takes a great deal of sacrifice, maturity, selflessness, and love to truly live out our wedding vows. Chesterton writes, ". . . it is this transfiguring self-discipline that makes the vow a truly sane thing."[3]

A Relationship with God

The second tool needed for couples to truly live out their wedding vows is a relationship with God. You who are married may have discovered by now that it takes more than self-discipline to live out your wedding vows. Our love is finite, but God's love is infinite. Our love has limits, but God's love has none. "It is no longer I but Christ who lives in me."[4] If Christ's love lives in our marriage, then it will thrive! This is why a couple's continued interaction with a church community is so crucial. It is this interaction with the church community that can help to deepen the relationship with the Author of love and marriage. Many couples coming forward to be married in any church do not have a substantial relationship with God. It is up to you to help them to deepen that relationship by inviting them to church, to couple events, and to any opportunity that has the potential to draw them deeper into a relationship with God. The effect of your relationship with God will impact them as a couple.

If you and your spouse are not on the same page regarding the importance of having a deep and personal relationship with God the Father, Son, and Holy Spirit, this may present a challenge as you minister to young couples. It is important to come together in this, foremost for your own marriage. You may want to share with your couples that this is an area in which you are still growing as a couple, and let them know how you support and pray for each other.

One of the simplest, and most grace-filled, ways of growing in relationship with God is to read Scripture with your spouse. Read it, pray about it, discuss it, and pray about it some more. The Word of God is alive and active and able to discern the thoughts of men.[5] Simply praying and sharing together is a concrete and tangible way of inviting God into your marriage and your relationship. If the couple you are mentoring has some struggles and fears, it may be helpful for them to voice these in prayer. Encourage them to do so. There are some great resources for couple prayer listed in the resource section of this book.

Habits That Can Unite

The third tool that will help couples to make it through the tough times is learning habits that will help increase their chances of marital success. The habits that we bring into marriage can shape our marriage early on. They can set the tone for a couple's future together. Couples come to the altar with so many different habits, ways of responding to each other, personal preferences, fears, and expectations. There was a couple with whom we recently worked who told us that they were already discussing divorce a month after their wedding day. As the conversation unfolded, they admitted that they were each so fearful of being left by the other. Consequently, they were purposefully saying and doing hurtful things to each other and threatening to leave. This way they would be the one who did the leaving and not the one who was left. As they opened up and shared with each other their fears, they were able to connect on a much deeper level and begin to heal the rift in their marriage. This is an extreme example, but there are many times throughout the lifetime of a marriage that one or both spouses get in a rut and end up responding to each other in ways that they would never respond to a friend.

There are many reasons for these behaviors. Ultimately, no one goes into marriage planning to make his or her spouse miserable. The Gottman Institute conducted a study that involved more than 100 newlywed couples. It observed them and how they interacted with each other. The study showed that simply being kind to your spouse and taking note of the things that they invite you to notice or enjoy with them are two ways of ensuring that your marriage will last *and* also be a happy marriage.[6] This study found that one spouse either waited for their spouse to do something right and applaud it, or waited for the other to do something wrong and pounce on it. They classified these two types of couples as "masters," and "disasters." They then followed these couples over the years and found that they could predict marital failure or success with 95 percent accuracy. According to the study, a habit is developed. They said, "There's a habit of mind that the masters have, which is this: They are scanning the social environment for things they can appreciate and for which they can be thankful. They are building this culture of respect and appreciation very purposefully. Disasters are scanning the social environment for their partners' mistakes."[7] The moral of the story is to bring kindness to your marriage and to start every day with the habit of being kind to your spouse. How can that go wrong? Yes, it is hard to be kind when you are mad, but if one partner remains kind and calm, the disagreement can never escalate. The worst thing that they found in a relationship was contempt. "Contempt, they have found, is the number one factor that tears couples apart. People who are focused on criticizing their partners miss a whopping 50 percent of positive things their partners are doing, and they see negativity when it's not there. People who give their partner the cold shoulder—deliberately ignoring the partner or responding minimally—do damage to the relationship by making their partner feel worthless and invisible, as if they're not there. Those who treat their partners with contempt and criticize them, not only kill the love in the relationship, but *also kill their partner's ability* to fight off viruses and cancers. Being mean is the death knell of relationships.[8] If you are mentoring a couple, you may want to examine how kind you are in your conversations and daily interactions. If you need a "reset" and a plan to start over, have a conversation about it, and let your spouse know that you want to work every day to honor your wedding vows. Let your spouse know that you realize that sometimes the way you talk is not "cherishing" or "honoring." We all need to start fresh every day!

Remind your newlywed couple over and over again that when newlywed couples have their first argument or disagreement, they frequently will come crashing down. They feel that their "rose-colored glasses" have been shattered, and they are now seeing their spouse as they really are. "How could I have married such a selfish person?" they wonder.

This disillusionment happens to everyone. Why? Because each of us is married to a selfish person, and our spouse is married to a selfish person, too.

An article in the New York Times cited a study that found a couple's happiness before marriage was unrelated to how long the marriage lasted. "What counts in making a happy marriage is not so much how compatible you are, but how you deal with incompatibility."[9]

Sharing how you and your spouse worked through your incompatibilities will greatly relieve and enrich a newly-wed couple. You may have shared examples of this before the wedding, but now they are finally experiencing those incompatibilities. Prior to our marriage, we had only one disagreement. The conversation lasted hours. We could not resolve the issue. It was a source of disagreement for our first year or two of marriage. Now it is no longer an issue. Why? It was such a silly disagreement that it took us *only* two years of marriage to see it. At the center of almost every disagreement that a married couple has is the sense of disrespect and also a sense that our spouse does not have our best interest at heart. We prefer things one way; they prefer them another way. Therefore, they disrespect us; they do not honor our feelings; and in some way they dishonor us. Read that last sentence again. There is some truth to this. Usually your spouse just has a personal preference that was there even before becoming part of your life. A habit, for example, need not always be a negative thing. However, when two people are married, the habits you bring into marriage need to be reevaluated with your spouse's preferences in mind. Not everything has to be changed, but there may be a few key things that are important to your spouse. If you do not take note of them, your spouse will feel some degree of disrespect. Over time, your spouse will just come to accept some things, and may even find them endearing. However, there are other things that simply need to be addressed. These more bothersome or challenging habits or preferences will erode even the best of relationships if they are not addressed. Something we always tell couples, "In the end, is your personal preference worth the damage it could do to your marriage relationship?" When put in those terms, it makes those little things we do that annoy our spouse seem very solvable, and something that we should seriously consider changing. "Research . . . has shown that kindness (along with emotional stability) is the most important predictor of satisfaction and stability in a marriage."[10] It is out of kindness that we respect our spouse's preferences. It is out of a desire to live out authentically our wedding vows that we try again each day to love and to honor them more. To recap these studies, it is has been proven that living out your wedding vows will ensure that your marriage will have the greatest chance of success. If your spouse is doing the same thing, then you have a much greater chance of marital success, and not just a lasting marriage but also a happy one. So often when the wedding vows are exchanged at the altar, couples are so nervous that they barely know what they are saying. We always ask couples to recite their vows again together as a reminder of what they have promised. It is not just a promise made in the past, but one made daily for the present and the future.

During our first year of marriage we built a house, had a premature baby, lost a job, and had a rough recovery from a C-section. It was a long year. Ryan says the first year was the worst, but I suggested it was the hardest. We learned so much that first year that everything else has seemed easy in comparison. During the year after we were married, we stood on the banks of the Mississippi River and repeated our wedding vows to each other. We pondered together the readings from our wedding. After a year of trying to live out our vows, those words meant something very different than they had that beautiful spring morning when we had said, "I do." We now know that "I do" actually means "I do - today, and tomorrow, and every day for the rest of my life, no matter how hard it is." It is something to be said when it is a long, cold, rainy winter and you are struggling with postpartum depression. It is something to be said when you are so tired from work and life that you just want to sit in your car and not go home to your family. It is something to be said when your spouse wants to dance to a Frank Sinatra song just because it's on the radio. It is

> At the center of almost every disagreement that a married couple has is the sense of disrespect and also a sense that our spouse does not have our best interest at heart. We prefer things one way; they prefer them another way.

something to be said when you see your spouse and children flying a kite on a breezy summer evening, and you join them.

Eventually, you may have found that "I do" means "checking into life" instead of "checking out of life." It means living your marriage and not just enduring your marriage. It means listening to your spouse and noticing what he or she wants to share with you. If it is significant to your spouse, then it should be significant to you. There is a great example of this in a study on marriage that we referenced earlier:

> Throughout the day, partners would make requests for connection, what Dr. Gottman calls "bids." For example, say that the husband is a bird enthusiast and notices a goldfinch fly across the yard. He might say to his wife, "Look at that beautiful bird outside!" He's not just commenting on the bird here: he's requesting a response from his wife—a sign of interest or support—hoping they'll connect, however momentarily, over the bird.
>
> The wife now has a choice. She can respond by either "turning toward" or "turning away" from her husband, as Gottman puts it. Though the bird-bid might seem minor and silly, it can actually reveal a lot about the health of the relationship. The husband thought the bird was important enough to bring it up in conversation, and the question is whether his wife recognizes and respects that.[11]

What Dr. Gottman calls a "bid" is actually an opportunity to connect. If we cannot connect over the small things, then when stress or challenges come our way, we can so easily forget the small joys that we have shared. Instead of working together, we think only of ourselves. These "bids" are really

> Eventually, you may have found that "I do" means "checking into life" instead of "checking out of life." It means living your marriage and not just enduring your marriage.

a bidding to come outside of ourselves and to share what we delight in with our spouse. This is the joy of not being alone. You have someone with whom you can share the little things. If we are annoyed when they share these little things with us, then it is a great time to re-evaluate our attitude towards marriage and our spouse. A beautiful unity results where life and love connect. Unity bears fruit in your life and in the lives of all who interact with you.

The number one good of marriage is "unity." It is the great barometer of the health of a marriage, and a good tool to use in discernment about issues that come your way as a couple. This is a question we ask ourselves every day as a couple, "Is this invitation going to ultimately bring us closer together, or is it going to drive us apart?" Sometimes it is an easy decision, but sometimes it is extremely hard. It was more challenging to discern this question when we first got married, but we have discovered that finding the answer to this question is easy. However, following through is much harder!

Here is an example from our lives. Ryan needed to go to Washington D.C. for a week for work. We know many families who have jobs that take spouses away from one another for weeks or even months at a time. We knew that this would be a very long time for us as a family to be apart. We had so much going on but now we had this opportunity to go on a road trip as a family. It could have been a disaster! We tried not to argue over it and prayed about it for a few days. It seemed like a crazy thing to do, but the ultimate discernment came down to this: "Will we be closer as a family and as a couple at the end or not?" We thought of how easy it would be to not make the trip. Ryan could just fly up to D.C. for the week, go to work, meet up with old friends and then be home at the end of the week. While he was gone, Mary Rose would bring the kids to visit their friends and get a few things done around the house. Why couldn't we just be finished discerning this and move on? Sometimes doing the harder thing is the more unitive choice. In this case, we decided to go to D.C. as a family. As a result, we had the best trip, and it was rewarding and unifying as a couple and as a family. We had no regrets.

The takeaway from this story is not: "You, too, should take your children and spouse on a 1,000-mile road trip." Rather, it is this: "If something seems ridiculously hard, it doesn't mean it is not worth doing. It may have the potential to be unifying for your relationship." When you mentor a couple who is discerning some of those big items relating to houses, jobs, starting a family, or friendships, encourage them to discern and pray about the ways these decisions will bring them closer together. Being able to ask the tough questions has given us much peace and provided more direction for us as a couple.

Community with Like-Minded Couples

The fourth tool to help strengthen a couple's relationship is building community. When it came to building community and making "couple friends" after we were married, we used a very similar question to discern if the time we were spending with friends was beneficial. Once a couple gets married, and especially once they start having kids, they begin to "pair off" with other like-minded couples. They gravitate towards those couples who value, enjoy, and do the same things they do. They make time to hang out with those families with whom their kids have developed friendships. Over the years, deep friendships are formed between families. You may not have as many close friends as you once did, but there is a satisfaction in seeing that your family is enjoying another family who values what you value.

Sometimes God will challenge you to go outside your comfort zone of building community with like-minded couples and families and bond with a family with whom you are not already "old-friends." You can call this "family mentoring," and it happens all the time, but the fruits of family mentoring are much less obvious than couple mentoring. Family mentoring is much more organic and natural than couple mentoring. Just as families can pick up some bad habits from those with whom they associate, the same can be said for the good habits. You need to strike a balance when it comes to introducing your children to families whom you are just getting to know. This takes more discernment and wisdom than mentoring a newlywed couple. You may need to set some healthy boundaries as you get to know a new family.

One of the key reasons for building community is that when you face challenges in your marriage or as a family, there will be others to support and encourage you. We read in the book of Ecclesiastes, "For if they fall, one will lift up his fellow. But woe to him who is alone when he falls and has not another to lift him up!"[12] This is so important for married couples. When couples struggle with the loss of a child, sickness, infidelity, depression, substance abuse, or a loss of faith, they will have another couple to seek out for support.

Do not let the young couples in your community drift away from other families. Connect them to other great families. Invite them to continue going to church with you. Offer to help paint their house, make meals after the birth of a baby, or whatever else they might need. Don't assume that their family or other friends are helping out. You might be the only one offering. It is not just about helping them in their present moment of need, but also building a bridge of trust so that they can approach you in the future. It is much easier to reach out to someone when they have already been reaching out to you.

Does Mentoring End?

When the couple you have been mentoring finally walks away from that altar, do not think that your job is complete. It is just beginning. There are so many versions of marriage mentor ministries in the marketplace. The majority of them suggest that you let the couple know that you are not their friends but only mentors. They tell you to emphasize that mentors are to help only for a period of time. We are asking you to consider sharing your marriage and your lives with other couples who need your witness. We are asking you to share what you want them to see and what you would prefer not to share. We are inviting you to work on your marriage so that you can walk with others on this path to Heaven. We feel you need to walk with them not just for a few months but for as long as God wants you to be their mentors. Sometimes people move away and a distance is created. You still can send them cards and pray for them. They appreciate it more than you know. Do not let your wounded human nature get in the way. It is easy to become lazy when it comes to sustaining relationships. Ask God for the grace to continue walking with those couples that He has brought into your lives. It is easy to think: "I've contributed my share of time to this couple. Perhaps someone else should mentor them now. Maybe they don't need us anymore." If you really feel this way, make sure to pray hard about what God wants from you. God wants to use you to change lives not only before the wedding day, but also during the most difficult parts of their journey. This usually means being a part of their lives those first ten years after the wedding.

To sum up, we encourage you to continue to reach out and to strengthen them in their commitment to one another. Help them to build unitive habits. Invite them into community with you. Find creative ways to nurture and maintain that relationship between them and the faith community. Seek to form them into actively receiving and giving to the ecclesial community that leads them to a deeper relationship with God. It is a lot of work, but it is worth it.

Chapter 9

True Tales of Happily Ever After

WE mentioned earlier about how much we enjoy reading fairy tales to our five-year-old daughter. Have you noticed that almost every fairy tale ends with a welcoming cheer from the community as they celebrate the newly-married prince and princess? Every one of us has a God-given desire for good relationships and lasting friendships. Eternity has been placed in our hearts. When it comes to the married vocation, this applies even more. We were meant to say and to live "I do" until death separates us, and we were meant to live in community surrounded by those who love and support us. Marriage is not a fairytale, but the truths illustrated in these many familiar tales help to reveal the longing within each person to live in love and in community. This longing remains even among those whose marriages are broken by divorce. This longing remains even for those couples who have yet to experience true community and family life. Marriage is itself the original "community of persons,"[1] and healthy marriages form healthy communities. One of the greatest joys of our lives is our mission to walk with couples throughout their marriage preparation process. We would like to share with you a few stories about those couples with whom we have had the honor to walk. The names of these couples have been changed to safeguard their identity.

How God Brought a Couple to the Sacrament of Marriage

Earlier in this book, we introduced you to Jason and Kelly. They had known each other for many years, had dated off and on through college, and eventually married civilly. They had been married for five years when they decided that they wanted to have their marriage "blessed." They wanted a sacramental marriage. Approximately one third of the couples who come for sacramental marriage preparation at our church are civilly married. These kinds of marriage conversion stories are encouraging, but Jason and Kelly's story is especially so. Jason and Kelly had been trying to conceive a child during the entire time they were civilly married. They had spent a year's income on fertility treatments with no success. When they were scheduled to go in for what they had decided would be their last fertility treatment, Kelly became ill with the flu. The doctors advised her not to come in for the treatment because she had a high fever. Kelly and her husband decided that God was in control, and from that day forward they put their fertility and their marriage in God's hands. After letting go and giving it to God, Kelly became pregnant without ever having gone to the fertility appointment. Our point with their story is to show you how one couple came to desire sacramental marriage. God's working in their life through the gift of a child brought them to desire something more for their marriage.

We will never forget the summer night we sat with them on our back porch listening to Jason and Kelly's story. Their story had a deep impact on our understanding of how greatly God cares for every detail of our lives, but it also changed the way we interact with other couples. We realized that couples cannot desire what they do not know. Or if they do desire it, they do not know exactly what they desire. God worked in their lives and opened their hearts to His greater plan for them. We were able to participate in His plan. I remember the day before the blessing of their marriage Kelly sent me an email. It read, "I do not know which I am more excited about: receiving communion in a state of grace after all this time or experiencing our first "one flesh" union in a sacramental marriage." They were so excited to be able to receive the Eucharist again after years of not being in full communion. They were equally excited to be together in the marital embrace as a sacrament, blessed by God through the Church and as an avenue of grace for their mutual growth in the Holy Spirit.

We knew that God had done so much already without us. We were playing a small part in the way that he was caring for this couple and bringing them closer to Him through the sacrament of marriage. We realized that the grace of the sacrament can take what is good on a natural level and raise it to a whole new level. To quote Pope St. John Paul II, marriage is "an indissoluble communion that 'sinks its roots' in the natural complementarity that exists between man and woman, and is nurtured through the personal willingness of the spouses to share their entire life project, what they have and what they are."[2] Marriage is a life-long project wherein a couple gives all that they have and all that they are to live a life together that is rooted in their love for each other and their love for God. We have continued to interact with this couple over the years. It is a joy to see them and their family grow. They have become a blessing to others!

Can Coming from a Divorced Home Make a Marriage Stronger?

Beth and Damien were a vibrant, young, and attractive couple. They had just finished college and were applying to graduate schools. During the marriage preparation process, our pastor had asked Mary-Rose to be a "spiritual sister" to Beth and to help them to prepare for marriage. They lived a few hours away at college so Mary-Rose and Beth had many phone conversations so that there would be some relational mentorship forming until they could meet in person. The first time Mary-Rose and Beth met, a deep friendship began. During the course of marriage preparation, Beth and Damien decided to abstain until after their wedding vows and decided to use natural family planning. Beth shared that both her parents and Damien's

> Marriage is a life-long project wherein a couple gives all that they have and all that they are to live a life together that is rooted in their love for each other and their love for God.

parents were divorced, and that this brokenness presented a challenge to their hopes and dreams for a future family together. Later Beth and Damien shared this with us:

> Since a very young age, we began to view family and relationships as a prize to be cherished. Having your parents separate at a young age changes you as a person. For example, the combination of having to handle your own feelings and take care of siblings at the same time may cause you to grow up sooner than you anticipated. For us, it changed the way we viewed marriage and family. It was as if the hope for a happy and loving family was taken from us, wrapped neatly in a box, stored away in some far-off land, and couldn't be opened until later on in life.

For Beth and Damien their parents' divorces actually motivated them not to follow the path taken by their parents. They were especially concerned for the sake of their future children. Their dreams and desires for the many wonderful events and conversations that should take place within the life of a family were missing for them. This is both beautiful and tragic. There are many couples with whom we speak that identify with Damien and Beth's experience of having all of these joys taken away as children, but

> It was as if the hope for a happy and loving family was taken from us, wrapped neatly in a box, stored away in some far-off land, and couldn't be opened until later on in life.

somehow being able to experience them later in life after having a family of their own that is committed to sharing both the joys and the sorrows.

As their wedding day approached, their anticipation and desire to begin a family together grew stronger. It was as if getting married was the opening of that gift that had been taken away from them for a time. They explained:

> Suddenly, we began to feel closer to that hidden gift. All the chasing of this arbitrary gift only made our wedding day that much more special. It was the best day of our lives for many reasons. One reason was that we were finally able to discover and open that gift box. We were like five-year-olds on Christmas morning. Although we were happier than ever to have our cherished prize back, we knew there was work to be done. All of those tough years of parental divorce made us aware that this wasn't a lucky gift from some far-off land, but that it was one directly from the hand of God. It was a special gift that is only received by those who open their hearts and minds to a relationship with God. Our childhood pain will never let us view our marriage and family as anything less than a gift from God.

During the months after their wedding, they began graduate school and had to live in different cities for short periods of time. They grew as a couple and came to visit us when they could. Towards the end of their time in graduate school they began to discern starting a family. One day, as Mary-Rose was driving to the airport, Beth called and wanted to know, "How do you know when it is the right time to start your family?"They did not have jobs or a house, and were still finishing graduate school. They saw all their friends and siblings having babies. They talked often about conceiving a child. Mary-Rose asked Beth if they were able to explain how they knew it was the right time to conceive a child. If so, were they at peace with their decision? Ultimately, they realized they could wait a few more months to see if things would fall into place. Years ago, when Mary-Rose was discerning moving to Louisiana, her spiritual director said, "Where there is peace and joy--that is the direction you should go." Mary-Rose gave the same advice to Beth and Damien. A few months closer to graduation they were at peace with starting to try to conceive even though they did not have a job or a house yet. A few weeks later, they were expecting; soon after that they both had job offers and had bought a house. Again, it is so inspiring for us to see how faithfully and intimately God involves Himself in our lives if we allow Him! When you are mentoring couples, you cannot help but see it!

The Beauty of Being Asked to be Mentors

This last couple's journey is especially dear to us because they grew so much, and we were able to experience how grace can renew a relationship. Dan and Elise had been civilly married for a short time and had four children between them but no children together. They had a hard time finding their mentor couple, but when they did, they found a good one. They asked us to meet them at their mentors' home because they both had small children. Mary-Rose was nervous about going to meet with them for the first time to talk about how to share your marriage and get the most out of the marriage preparation process. The evening with the mentors and Dan and Elise turned out to be a wonderful time. They had picked some amazing friends to be their mentors. Halfway through their marriage preparation, Elise called to let us know that their mentors had some health issues come up and would not be able to finish the process, even though they would be able to reach out to them later on when the health crisis was over. Elise explained that she and Dan wanted us to be their mentors.

Our initial reaction was, "What? That is too much work for us. We are far too involved in so many things. How can we mentor another couple?" Our selfish reaction eventually changed to, "Wow! They were serious. No one had ever asked us to be their mentors. We were always assigned a couple to mentor, but no engaged couple had ever chosen us." We agreed to do it. We began meeting with them at our home to go over questions about all the life-skills issues, and we talked to them about their daily struggles, their desire for the sacrament of marriage, and what brought them to church. We were shocked when Dan responded that his years serving time in the penitentiary brought about his conversion. He spoke with tears in his eyes about how he had read Scripture in a prayer group. He said that all the other inmates said he would feel different about God when he got out. Dan was only more on fire with love for God when he got out of prison. He met Elise, got married and started going to church irregularly. Their children wanted their parents to be married in church, and they wanted to be baptized. During Easter that year their children were baptized and soon after finishing their marriage preparation, Dan and Elise were married in the church. They knew the gift of the sacrament they were receiving! They knew they were entering into a covenant and how different that was from their contracted "civil marriage." They were more prepared and excited than most couples who did everything in the "right" order.

A Second Class Sacrament?

Before the wedding day, we found out that Dan and Elise had invited a large number of friends and family to the ceremony. We had expected it to be a small affair since they had already been civilly married. In many churches, the custom is to keep the ceremony small and simple. They asked us to attend the wedding, and we were honored to be asked. The wedding ceremony was very humble, but it was one of the most beautiful weddings we have witnessed! Dan and Elise's joy, along with their children's joy, was contagious. Since we had spent time discussing the meaning of the sacrament of marriage with them and our pastor over dinner, listened to their conversion story, prayed with them and for them, Dan and Elise's wedding was a deeply moving moment for us.

We came to realize that there is no such thing as a second-class sacrament. Their friends (many of whom were not married) were able to witness Dan and Elise's joy and listen to our pastor explain every aspect of the ceremony to them. No doubt, their friends were able to be exposed to something they would not have been exposed to if we had asked Dan and Elise to "keep it small." We are so glad that they invited us and so many others to share in their joy!

Since then, our friendship has deepened with Dan and Elise. Recently, we invited them to a couple's retreat with us, but they had to turn us down because they had already committed to another couple's retreat the same weekend! Their marriage is alive and thriving, and we have the on-going blessing of being a part of their lives. The journeys of these three couples continue to have an impact on us as we watch God work in their marriages to bring them to a true happily ever after.

Chapter 10

The Shared Fruits of the Mentor Model

THE fruits of mentoring are not just one-sided. These fruits are shared among the whole community, the engaged couple's family, and the mentors themselves. We have found that engaged couples tend to choose mentors who are truly a providential match for them. Mentors share with us that they receive far more than they give to the engaged couple and we too have found this to be true in our own mentor relationships. We witness greater expectations from engaged couples as they approach the process of preparing for marriage. The tangible fruits of mentoring continue to surprise us.

A Providential Match

We ask our engaged couples to choose their own mentors, and we offer to coach these couples about how to mentor. Jerry and Rhonda were one of the first mentors that an engaged couple brought to our door a few years ago. We asked the engaged couple to share with them the reasons they chose them as their mentors. The engaged couple explained how much they admired Jerry and Rhonda as a couple and were impressed with how close they were as a family. Jerry and Rhonda became emotional when they were told how much their mentorship would mean. At the time, we did not understand why they became so emotional.

A few years later Jerry and Rhonda were once again being asked to be mentors by another engaged couple. This time Jerry and Rhonda were glowing and confident. They were so excited to be mentors. The new couple they were mentoring had many challenges and issues with trust, forgiveness, and honesty. As we coached Jerry and Rhonda to share their marriage with Brent and Ashley, something beautiful happened. Rhonda shared how a few years prior many of her friends were going through divorce. She was sure she and Jerry would be next. She kept looking for something to go wrong. One day she saw a message he had sent to a female coworker. There was nothing unusual or wrong with the message, but she did not bring it up to him and obsessed over it for a month. Rhonda began to dream up stories about Jerry and his co-worker in her head. Their intimacy stopped. Jerry had no idea what was going on because Rhonda would not say. Finally, after a month, she confronted him about the message. He could not believe that was the cause of everything. They realized their fear of divorce was pushing them towards it. They chose to stay committed and honest with each other, and their love was renewed. We found out that the first time we met them was just days after their misunderstanding about the message had been resolved.

Now God was using them to speak to Brent and Ashley who themselves were struggling to trust and to be honest with each other. Jerry and Rhonda's story moved Ashley and Brent to completely open up. We could see immediately that the friendship and mentorship between these two couples was providential. We never could have ministered to Ashley and Brent in the ways they needed. Jerry and Rhonda were able to share the unhappiness of what they had endured and overcome effectively and fruitfully. We can see how much Jerry and Rhonda have grown in their marriage since the first meeting we had with them years ago. They have become such a treasure to many other couples.

The Church's Greatest Resource is You

There are recurring comments we hear almost every time we welcome an engaged couple and their mentor couple into our home. The mentors always want to know why they never had this kind of marriage preparation when they were getting married. "If we had this kind of preparation, we would have avoided so much heartache! We missed out!" They are always so glad to know that the church is finally doing something that makes so much sense. We then have to explain that we are only one of a few churches doing marriage preparation this way. The majority of clergy with whom we speak are interested in how we do marriage preparation and the use of mentors, but they worry that they will never be able to find volunteers. The church needs YOU! Without married couples helping our clergy, they can do only so much. A church community that is not making use of its greatest resources (married couples) is missing out on a beautiful renewal. We have seen, and continue to see, so many grace-filled friendships formed in our church. These friendships are spilling out into neighboring churches, as some couples live in different towns than their mentors.

Greater Expectations

The expectations of marriage preparation have changed in our community. We found this out the hard way. Father Michael, our pastor, had a couple come to him. They were in a long distance relationship and both lived out of town. He decided that it would be too hard for this couple do what all of our couples do for marriage preparation, so he decided just to send them to a one-day conference for engaged couples. They quickly became very upset and begged that they receive the same kind of marriage preparation that their cousin had received. They wanted a mentor! They said, "This is our time. We need this. We want the works. We want everything you have to give us!" Couples now know about our marriage preparation program, and they *want* it! This makes it so much more rewarding to work with them. We are all working for the same thing—strong marriages.

> The church needs YOU! Without married couples helping our clergy, they can do only so much. A church community that is not making use of its greatest resources (married couples) is missing out on a beautiful renewal.

Another couple that we prepared for marriage prior to allowing couples to pick mentors came back to us. They wanted to know why they did not get the full marriage preparation. We explained that they were the last couple we had worked with before realizing that couples needed to choose a mentor couple. The husband stated very seriously that he wished he had the preparation that his brother had just completed. His brother was recently married in our church. The older brother told us that if he had received what his younger brother had, then he and his wife would be in a much better place. They had gone through some rough times and would have given anything to have a mentor in their lives. It is not just those who are getting married who need mentors. Married couples need mentors too.

Fruits Worth Sharing

The fruits of mentoring are being shared with the whole community. We have been stopped by the parents of couples we have helped to prepare, and they always say, "Thank you for giving our children a preparation that we never had." There are so many beautiful fruits that come from allowing engaged couples to partner with couples they admire. Here are a few of them:

- ◊ Through this process, we are forming the future of our church by forming more families who understand and are prepared to live out their vocation.

- We have civilly married couples who had children already asking for us to give them resources to speak to their kids about human sexuality/Theology of the Body while we were doing their marriage preparation.
- We have Sponsors/Mentors becoming religious education teachers, lectors, Extraordinary Ministers of Holy Communion, prayer group leaders, youth group volunteers, men's group and women's group leaders and participants.
- Our mentors and engaged couples are attending parish events together. Something none had done before.
- Our mentors desire to keep serving the Church and want to know more about their faith!
- Established Married Couples now have an avenue through which to share the fruits of their marriages. As the Sponsor/Mentor couples are formed and share their experiences, their marriages grow.
- Mentors are often asked to be the godparents.
- Mentored couples take more of an interest in truly raising their children in the faith.

These are just some of the more obvious fruits of mentoring, but there are many more that are not visible to the observer. These other fruits we only know about because couples have shared them with us. They are:

- A renewal of the mentor couple's marriage and a new appreciation for their sacrament of marriage.

- ◇ An openness to having more children due to a deeper understanding of the gift of life.
- ◇ Better communication with their spouse about important matters because they have to prepare to share their marriage with another couple.
- ◇ A deeper relationship with God because they see clearly how He is working in the engaged couple's life.

We have seen and experienced all of these fruits even in our own marriage.

There is No Perfect Time to Share Your Marriage

Every engaged couple and every mentor couple who have come through our doors over the years have been a blessing to us. Always, and without fail, the nights they come are at the end of the craziest and most draining days. We are exhausted, and the kids are not putting on their best faces. We worry that the engaged couple will see the chaos and decide that marriage is not for them. We worry that perhaps they have chosen a mentor couple that is less than helpful. We wonder why God would want two people as ordinary as us to take on such a tremendous task.

We sit down with the couples regardless of the craziness and chaos of family life going on around us. A recent mentor observed that one time when she was at our house our eldest was wearing a pull up and dancing in a puddle in our driveway. She remembered this and shared it with the engaged couple. We are not sure if she was trying to tell them it could be worse or if it was just a fond memory. Couples are so excited and hungry to be fed the truth. It doesn't

> It doesn't matter to them if the domestic scene is less than ideal. In fact, they actually seem to enjoy it. Rather than being turned off by the chaos, they see that this is what they have to look forward to in family life.

matter to them if the domestic scene is less than ideal. In fact, they actually seem to enjoy it. Rather than being turned off by the chaos, they see that this is what they have to look forward to in family life. Ultimately, that is the point! God can use us as instruments and mentors, only if we are humble and allow Him to do it. We allow Him in by opening up our hearts and our homes to those who are preparing for the blessing and challenge of marriage. Open the doors to your domestic church. You will be awed by the blessings that follow.

Chapter 11

A Special Vocation: Saving Troubled Marriages

MICHELLE and Kenneth recently shared with us that they were discussing the possibility of a divorce. As the conversation unfolded, they admitted that they were so fearful of being left by the other that they were purposefully saying and doing things to hurt one another. Their threats of divorce were tearing their marriage apart. We asked them what their greatest fear was, and they told us, "Our greatest fear is being left by the other." We let them know that they had everything to gain and nothing to lose if they would do just one thing each day to help sustain their marriage. Michelle and Kenneth had never prayed together before. We asked them to hold hands, turn to one another, and repeat these words, "I love you and I will never leave you. I love you, and I do not want to hurt you. I am sorry for the times that I have hurt you. Please forgive me. I want to love you as God created you to be loved." The tears poured down their cheeks. They asked if they could get a pen and paper to write these words down. They stated that they had never at any time in their relationship felt as close and as safe as they did at that moment. Ryan often reminds me of the saying, "Hurt people hurt people." This means that those who have been hurt or are hurting will often hurt others. They lash out. They do not want to be hurt again. In marriage this takes the form of saying or doing things that look like they are being done to push the other spouse away or hurt them.

Breaking the Cycle of Hurt

In many of these cases the hurt spouse is "testing" the love of the other. They want to know that they will not be left and will be loved. They push the other away in hopes that they will be embraced. This makes no sense to someone who has never been deeply wounded. However, to those who are wounded, it is a means of survival. They carry a chip on their shoulder that says, "Prove you love me. Prove that even I am lovable." When they do things that are unlovable and their spouse responds with threats of leaving, as in the earlier example, then the hurt spouse becomes even more convinced of their "un-lovableness." If both spouses are hurting one another, then saving that marriage is truly a miracle. One spouse must break the cycle of hurting. Without the grace to overcome one's personal (and very natural) feelings of anger and resentment towards the spouse who is rubbing salt in your wounds, divorce seems inevitable. If you see this pattern in a couple you are mentoring, or another couple that you come to know, then encourage them to break the cycle of hurt through the use of a mentor program like "Marriage Savers." Do not just let them be. Invite them to church. Introduce them to couples from whom they might learn something new. Share your marriage with them. Help them to identify and work through their challenges.

You Are That Credible Witness

If you have worked through a rough patch in your own marriage, you have much wisdom to offer to a struggling couple. As we go through trials in our own lives and storms in our own marriages, we will find later in life that God puts particular people in our paths because of our past experiences. In these moments God wants to use us to strengthen or assist another person. There is a reason for everything that we endure. When we come out on the other side of a difficulty that we have survived, we find that the fruit of our suffering has the ability to produce grace and healing in another person's life. This is true on both a natural level and a spiritual level. Think about Jesus' crucifixion. Remembering Christ's passion during times of sickness or pain can give us comfort and help us open up to Him.

It is a very similar phenomenon when it comes to working with couples in troubled marriages. If you have survived a troubled marriage, then you are a credible witness. If you know what it is like to go through anger and resentment and hurt with your spouse and come out on the other side in a thriving marriage, then you have something of value to share! Couples know they can open up their hearts and their pain to you. You can pray with them, and for them, and share with them the lessons of your past, the experience of forgiveness, and healing. You can help them to be accountable as they progress towards healing.

If you are a couple who has survived a troubled marriage, present yourself to your pastor or to those in your community who work with couples in troubled marriages. Let them know you are available to be mentors. If you are open to being trained to coach a couple in a troubled marriage, take the time to be equipped to do it. Pray about it and discuss it with your spouse if you feel called to be this kind of mentor. Become educated about the resources that are available, including those listed in the appendix of this book.

Not everyone is called to work closely with a couple who is experiencing challenges in their marriage, but all of us are called to pray for those who are hurting. Never underestimate the power of prayer. Christ who is the Author of marriage has the ability to heal and restore what appear to be doomed relationships. Time and time again when we pray with couples and encourage them to pray, we see that this has far more impact on the relationship then we could have anticipated.

When You do Not Know the Person You Are Married To

The situation of the couple we described earlier is more likely to be found in a marriage of ten years or less. What we see in couples married for longer than ten years is that they are disconnected from each other. They are neither hot nor cold but have simply drifted apart. These couples are much more challenging because often one or both of them have given up on the marriage. One or both are already saying to others how disappointed they are that they chose to waste their life with this person. Often they will say things like, "I feel like I don't even know this person." They got married, finished a degree, had children, and had a career. Then, usually around the time the children leave home, or when one or both of them retire, they realize that they do not really know the person that they've been living with for twenty, thirty, or more years. They grew apart because they did not spend enough time with each other over the years. They lived life more as acquaintances and less as lovers, more as parents and less as spouses. They were more focused on getting ahead than getting connected with one another.

One summer when I (Mary-Rose) was traveling on an airplane with one of our children, I found myself sitting next to a very quiet passenger who was not enjoying the sweet sounds of our daughter. I tried to give this slightly disgruntled passenger every benefit of the doubt as to why she might not like a cooing baby. I dreamed up every possible scenario in my head as to why she might be the way she was. After our baby had become obsessed with this woman's jewelry, the stone-faced passenger finally acknowledged that we were sitting next to her. She really had no choice. We began small talk about kids and babies, and the woman mentioned that she had grandchildren. I noticed that she was not wearing a wedding ring and was reading a steamy romance novel. Her grandmotherly appearance and strange attitude towards children was baffling. About halfway through the flight she asked me where I was going. I told her I was going to give a talk. "What's the topic?" she wanted to know. "Marriage," I responded. I saw a strange look come over her face. For the remainder of the flight, she proceeded to share her life story with me.

She shared that she was on her way to visit her children and grandchildren. The reason she was traveling to visit them was that she could not bear to live near her ex-husband who had deeply hurt her. I realized that the strange look on her face was actually pain. She said that less than a year ago she had finally retired, and she and her husband had finished putting their last child through college. She always thought they had a good relationship. For the past thirty years they had worked and planned for their retirement. Soon after she retired, her husband decided he needed to get out of the house. He frequently came and left, and she thought nothing of it. A month later she found out that he was having an affair. She confronted him and told him she wanted to work through it. He surprised her by stating that he was glad she found out, and he was ready to get out of their marriage. That same day he packed up his things, moved in with the other woman, and later married her. Now her children and her ex-husband wanted her to get over it and consider sharing the holidays with them. She had moved away so she would not have to see her husband of 40 years now living with another woman. How deep the wound of divorce is! Divorce is not natural. Jesus said that it was due to the hardness of their hearts that Moses allowed divorce, but in the beginning it was not so.[1]

Resurrecting a Marriage

We have known quite a few friends who have gone through rough times in their marriages and made it through these trials. The majority of them now have very strong relationships with each other and amazing relationships with their children. Nothing in life is easy, but giving up never makes anything truly better, especially when it comes to marriage! We all are going to suffer, struggle, fight, and become anxious about the meaning of our marriage at some point in time. That is normal. When anger and fighting between spouses becomes a weekly or even daily occurrence, it means they need help and hope, not a way out of the marriage. The marriage where a couple is fighting can still be saved. It is the couple who have already accepted the fact that the marriage is over who will have the greatest challenge. They discuss their relationship as if it were something already dead and buried. They have prematurely mourned it and have moved on in the journey of life. It is almost impossible to convince a couple in this situation that their marriage is "not dead but only sleeping."[2] Here it would take a miracle to raise this marriage from apparent death. Ultimately it takes grace, healing, and the hand of God, who joined this couple together in the first place, to bring their marriage back to a full life.

These couples need to be surrounded by a community of family, friends, mentors, and witnesses to love. Sadly, they are usually isolated or surrounded by well-meaning friends who are also mourners at the death of their marriage. Many of them have the how-to-manual on how to divorce easily ready to go! Instead, they should be yelling, "Wait, don't bury your marriage. Don't give up on your spouse. Your marriage may look like it is dead but it is not!" If you have friends, especially close ones, who are preparing to go through a divorce, encourage them to work it out rather than renounce their vows.

"Throw Away the Divorce Parachute"

One of our friends found out that his wife was cheating on him. She wanted to leave once he found out, but he wanted to work it out. They did work it out because of his persistence and willingness to forgive. They wanted to honor their vows rather than take the path that all of their friends suggested. Everyone around them had encouraged them to get divorced. When they went to their church for help, the counselor gave them a handout to help explain divorce to their children. No one—not even at their church—encouraged them to work it out! Many years later they still receive calls from husbands or wives who are considering divorce. Because this couple found Christ and healing in their marriage, their advice to other couples who are on the brink of divorce is always, "Throw away that parachute!

> When you open the door to the possibility of divorce as a solution to your problem, then a couple focuses on divorce, rather than focusing on saving the marriage!

There is only one door out—marriage. Do not ever, ever, ever, ever, ever, ever give up. Period." When you open the door to the possibility of divorce as a solution to your problem, then a couple focuses on divorce, rather than focusing on saving the marriage!

The question to ask couples considering divorce: "Is your spouse worth suffering for?" If the answer is "No," then ask them, "Was your spouse ever worth suffering for, and if so, when did that change?" When we get married, we are saying that we believe we have found someone worth suffering for. When you suffer for someone you love, it is redeeming and life giving. We don't get married to irritate the person we love (although it is bound to happen). We get married so that we are not suffering through life alone, so that we become more human and fully alive. C. S. Lewis writes this about men and women:

> There is, hidden or flaunted, a sword between the sexes till an entire marriage reconciles them. It is arrogance in us to call frankness, fairness, and chivalry "masculine" when we see them in a woman; it is arrogance in them, to describe a man's sensitiveness or tact or tenderness as "feminine." But also what poor, warped fragments of humanity most mere men and mere women must be to make the implications of that arrogance plausible. Marriage heals this. Jointly the two become fully human.[3]

Working through our human frailties in marriage with another person who also has the same frailties is impossible if done alone. Thank God for the gift of His grace and for those people He puts in our lives who reach out to us at just the right time! Be that instrument of God's grace for couples who are hurting. How do you know if you are called to help these couples? If you know a couple in this situation, then you are called to help. You may not be called to be their counselor, but you may be called to be a mentor, an intercessor, and a friend. Standing by and watching someone you know go through a divorce should never be an option.[4]

Relationships Grow Under the Shelter of Commitment

Where there is commitment, love will flourish and grow no matter what the challenges. The Irish priest we mentioned in chapter 8 also added a line that didn't sound quite right the first time we heard it. He said, it is not love that shelters a family but commitment. In the end it is the parents' commitment to each other that is going to be the main thing, the covering, that provides the roof over the family. It is the shelter that gives a family the ability to grow and be healthy. Children need to see that commitment more than anything else. At first we thought he was putting the cart before the horse, but he was right! Prior to marriage you have love, and then you commit. After marriage you are committed, and therefore, you love. Without commitment you cannot have love in marriage. The love you have for your spouse ultimately changes after your vows. It raises the stakes. For example, if a couple is dating but not yet engaged, they might think about a previous significant other. There is no sin in keeping your options open while dating. Once a couple is engaged it becomes a gray area. However, once a couple is committed in marriage, there is no longer any gray area—it becomes black and white. You have one spouse. That's it until death do you part. Giving yourself or some-one else "permission" to consider divorce is like saying, "You are right. Yours is a special case. God hadn't thought of a situation like yours when He said marriage was until death." Be careful that you do not appear to be giving this kind of advice.

—————◇—————

Prior to marriage you have love, and then you commit. After marriage you are committed, and therefore, you love. Without commitment you cannot have love in marriage. The love you have for your spouse ultimately changes after your vows. It raises the stakes.

—————◇—————

Becoming a Resource for Your Community

Again, if you have been through a difficulty in your marriage, you may want to consider being a resource for your community. Consider getting some training in a program like Prepare-Enrich, Marriage Savers, Alexander House or some similar ministry that helps churches and communities reach out to those in troubled marriages. If God has allowed you to experience trials in your marriage, perhaps He allowed it so that you might lift up those who have fallen. St. Paul says, "Blessed be the God and Father of our Lord Jesus Christ, the Father of compassion and God of all encouragement, who encourages us in our affliction, so that we may be able to encourage those who are in any affliction with the encouragement with which we ourselves are encouraged by God."[5]

Chapter 12

Marriage: A Glimpse of Heaven

Since we are surrounded by so great a cloud of
witnesses, let us rid ourselves of every burden and sin
that clings to us and persevere in running the race
that lies before us.[1]

- St. Paul's Letter to the Hebrews

If the gift of marriage really is "the one thing not washed
away in the flood,"[2] could we not say with confidence that
it might be the best way to direct us to Heaven? Consider
those times when you and your spouse are totally in sync, or
when the communication between you is wide open. Like-
wise, recall those times when you are transparent with each
other and working towards the same goals. These moments,
and those when you would do anything for love of each
other, you are united in your journey toward Heaven. These
times, don't you feel closest to God? More than a feeling,
you just know that God is loving you through your spouse.
You can feel His presence in your life and you notice the
ways that He is intimately involved in your day-to-day life.

Your spouse is your other half, your helpmate,[3] your companion, and together your lives are the original song that men and women were meant to sing to their Maker. This is God's original plan for marriage. Nothing more, and nothing less. Sadly, we, not God, have created the battle between the sexes, have declared that men and women are from different planets (Mars and Venus), and in every other way have convinced ourselves that we can never really understand one another and we can never be a team.

What is the first thing that happened after Adam and Eve shared in the first sin? They questioned God's goodness. The blame game began. The original unity between men and women was severely wounded. Christ came, in part, to give us the grace to live out the Sacrament of Marriage. Prior to Christ's coming, marriage was a not a sacrament. Men and women had to fight much harder to keep their marriages intact. (We discussed this in Chapter 1.) Today we have the grace of Jesus Christ, but we are not fully tapping into that grace given to us by God as a wedding gift!

Settling for a Mediocre Marriage vs. Marriage as a Vocation

When things get difficult, we settle for a mediocre marriage. We need to be reminded continually that there is nothing in God's plan that calls us to mediocrity. If marriage is your vocation, then settling for something less than what God wants for you means that you are not living out your vocation. There is a difference between staying married and recognizing marriage as your vocation. We must never settle and say, "We have a better marriage than most, so we are just fine." It is often said, with reference to the spiritual life, that we are always moving either closer to God or further away from God; there is no settling for the status quo. The Church Fathers have written this about our relationship with God, but it can also be said of your marriage. Either you are moving closer to God and to your spouse, or you are moving further away from God and from your spouse. There is no static state.

> We need to be reminded continually that there is nothing in God's plan that calls us to mediocrity. If marriage is your vocation, then settling for something less than what God wants for you means that you are not living out your vocation.

What couples mistake for "settling" in relationships is often actually indifference or isolation. We may not currently be thinking of leaving our spouses, but when we "settle" we are not actively doing anything to get them and us to Heaven. We are not making the most of the grace that is always new and abundant for us each day. God is not stingy with grace! He pours it over us each day. Depending on our openness to Him, we can let it roll off our backs like a duck, or we can soak it up like a sponge. Like the seed that fell on good soil in the Parable of the Sower (Matthew 13), let us live our marriages in such a way that we become the good soil and not the soil filled with rocks or thorns.

Marriages neither succeed nor fail overnight. Every day we wake up with an attitude that either helps to strengthen our marriage and the marriages of those around us, or we live in such a way that our marriages are taken for granted. Do not simply share your marriage, but take the time to discuss, examine, and pray about what you need to do as a couple to bring your marriage to the fullness that God wants for you. Some questions to help you to identify what area(s) of your marriage may need renewal:

◇ Are we actively living out our wedding vows?

◇ When is the last time we made a retreat together?

◇ Do we say "please," "thank you," and "forgive me" often, or are we stingy with these words?[4]

◇ Do we actively share our time and our marriage with others?

◇ Has work, kids, health, or life overwhelmed our relationship?

◇ When is the last time we went out on a real date? If it has been more than two months then close this book and take your spouse out!

◇ When is the last time we read and discussed a book together?

◇ How did our last disagreement end?

◇ When was the last time we thanked each other for something we normally do each day?

◇ Do we share our dreams for the future?

◇ How often do we just hug or hold hands for no reason?

- ◇ Do we miss each other when we are apart?
- ◇ When was the last time we prayed together, aside from grace before meals or at church?

These things may seem small, but actually they are not. Take time to discuss these with your spouse.

In our world we take so much for granted, and there are too many opportunities for marriage to operate like a business partnership. You go away for work, you balance the budget, you get your kids out the door, you take a break for meals, and every day is just another day. Whether it is a good or bad day, you get through it. God wants more for you! Remember the woman on the airplane who was married for 40 years and at retirement her marriage ended? Be sure to make time for each other even when there seems to be no time. As your marriage flourishes, you will build up a reservoir of grace that will begin to spill over onto those other couples that you know. Make sure you pray together so that your reservoir does not run dry.

The Marriage Mentor Action Plan

Here is where you can discuss an action plan for you and your spouse to begin sharing your marriage. As we said earlier, do not wait for your marriage to be "perfect" in your eyes before you begin to share it with others.

- ◇ Get involved at your church – ask what you can do to help.
- ◇ Become trained in some form of marriage preparation, support, or enrichment.

- ◇ Reach out to young adults and newly married couples that you know.
- ◇ Read and share the books in the Resources section of this book.
- ◇ Subscribe to some of the websites listed and share their articles on social media.
- ◇ Dust off your wedding photos and put them out for others to see.
- ◇ Reconnect with your children and their spouses if they are married.
- ◇ Revisit all the lists of questions in this book.
- ◇ Take the "Couple Checkup" or something like it (see Resources).
- ◇ Identify what you need to work on in your marriage and together come up with a game plan to work on it.
- ◇ Set a time each week to check in and see how you are doing.
- ◇ Identify a couple that you look up to and ask them to mentor you.
- ◇ Look at all the young couples with whom you interact and pray about the possibility of actively sharing your marriage with them, and discuss what steps you would take to begin.
- ◇ Visit elderly relatives and friends you know who have lost a spouse.
- ◇ Cook a meal for a couple who has just had a child.
- ◇ Reach out to that couple you know who is considering divorce.

◇ Discern what your couple "marriage mission" is
   – why did God bring you together and what do
   you have to share with others?
◇ If you knew your spouse had only one day left
   to live, what would be the thing you would
   want to say to them that you don't always say?
   Say it to them today and every day.
◇ If you are not actively a part of your church,
   become active now – being unplugged from the
   Body of Christ means there is a limit to what
   you will be able to share with others.
◇ Set aside time to pray with your spouse every
   day – begin by using something like "The Couple Prayer Series" (see Resources).
◇ Ask if there is a need for marriage prep teachers in your area. (Catholics, call your Diocesan
   Office of Marriage and Family Life.)

Pope Francis said to an audience of journalists, "Build a
culture of encounter. This is a fine task for you. This requires you
to be willing not only to give, but also to receive from others."[5]
While this was directed towards media personnel, it is a great
statement for all of us to remember. Go out and encounter others! Open yourself to others so that you might give *and* receive.

Watching God at Work

We have received so much more from working with
couples than we will ever be able to give back. We have
watched the hand and the heart of God working through

the lives of so many men and women as they learn to love as their hearts were created to love. We have watched half-hearted relationships bloom under the flood of grace that they received when they opened themselves up to the sacrament of marriage. Our lives are forever changed by the witness to love that we experience over and over again in our encounter with others who are living out their wedding vows.

Our prayer for you is that you will become a glimpse of Heaven for those who know you, and a living invitation to bring others closer to the heart of Christ. In His prayer to His Father, Christ prayed, ". . . that they may all be one; even as You, Father, are in Me and I in You, that they also may be in Us, so that the world may believe that You sent Me. The glory which You have given Me I have given to them, that they may be one, just as We are one."[6] It is in Christ that you will ultimately experience the unity with the Father that you were created for, and it is marriage that prepares you for that unity. If you live in Him, the glory of God will shine in you and lead other couples to unity with the Father.

> This is our vocation as Christians. This is our vocation in marriage. Lead our spouse to Christ and to lead others to Christ. We have an awesome mission and a great gift!

This is our vocation as Christians. This is our vocation in marriage. Lead our spouse to Christ and to lead others to Christ. We have an awesome mission and a great gift! Christ said to go out in twos as we spread the good news (Mk. 6:7). As we focus on being more united to Christ as a couple, we cannot help but unite others to Him as well. In the final scene of our favorite musical, "Les Misérables," the main character Jean Valjean is taking his final breath. At the same time he is being welcomed into Heaven by Fantine, the woman whom Valjean had protected and cared for during her last days on earth. She was a woman ignored and taken advantage of during her short life. Valjean loved Fantine with dedication, and he cared for

> When we love someone else with a sacrificial love, that we are beholding the very countenance of the Father and reflecting that same expression of love.

the little girl she left behind when she died. This once forgotten woman now welcomes Jean Valjean into paradise. It is in this final moment that Valjean realizes that when we love someone else with a sacrificial love, that we are beholding the very countenance of the Father and reflecting that same expression of love. When we love with the love of God, we enrich our own marriages, and grace and love will pour out into the lives of those around us. We are called to show the love of God and to behold the love of God in our marriage.

"No one has greater love than this, that someone would lay down his life for his friends" (John 15:13). While you may not physically have to die for your spouse or for the couples whom you are mentoring, God invites you daily to lay down your lives and your marriage at the feet of Christ.

It is your greatest gift as a couple. Share that gift. Sharing your marriage is the one thing that you can do together to bring this world back to understanding, accepting, and living the true meaning of holy married love.

A Note to Clergy

THE premise of this effort is based upon the fact that marriage preparation is successful if and when a couple is integrated into the life of the church/parish community. This is indicated consistently in every study and directive issued regarding the renewal of the marriage preparation process. A good friend of ours stated, "Marriage Preparation that does not successfully integrate engaged couples into the life of their church/parish has ultimately failed." We agree. When we prepare couples for marriage, we may never see them again or know how their marriages turned out. They use the church for their wedding but may never fully integrate into the faith community. How can you change this starting today? Read this book. Give a few copies to potential mentor couples in your church. Gather these couples and form a Marriage Ministry Team. Get trained in "Witness to Love," or find a way to use marriage mentors in your marriage preparation process.

If you currently use assigned mentor couples in your parish, you can greatly enhance that process. Use this book as a way to aid the assigned mentor couple in "passing the baton." The engaged couple can select a mentor couple whom they admire. At various points in the marriage preparation process, your assigned and already trained mentor couples can involve the selected couple whom the engaged couple already trusts and admires. In this way, the odds are in your favor for continued faith-based relationships, not only between the couples, but also with your church community. If your church is especially large or spread out, "Witness to Love" can have a unifying impact on your community.

This is two-for-one evangelization and marriage enrichment for the mentor couples. Ultimately, the payoff is tremendous. As you begin to focus on the marriage preparation process as an opportunity for evangelization, marriage discipleship, community-building, and church growth, you will find that God will bless your church community abundantly! To join the marriage preparation renewal movement visit: www.WitnesstoLove.org.

> As you begin to focus on the marriage preparation process as an opportunity for evangelization, marriage discipleship, community-building, and church growth, you will find that God will bless your church community abundantly!

Notes

Introduction

1 John Paul II, *Redemptor Hominis,* Vatican Translation, (Boston: Pauline Books and Media, 1979), no. 10.

Chater 1

1 Nuptial Blessing A, in *The Roman Missal,* trans. The International Commission on English in the Liturgy, 3rd typical ed., For the Celebration of Marriage, (Washington D.C.: United States Catholic Conference of Bishops, 2011), 1181.

2 Ibid., 1181.

3 John Paul II, "Homily: Apostolic Pilgrimage To Bangladesh, Singapore, Fiji Islands, New Zealand, Australia And Seychelles," Vatican Website, November 30, 1986, no. 4, accessed November 28, 2014, http://w2.vatican.va/content/john-paul -ii/en/homilies/1986/documents/hf_jp-ii_hom_19861130 _perth-australia.html.

4 Paul Strand, "Divorce Shocker: Most Marriages Do Make It," *CBN News US,* May 6, 2014, accessed November 19, 2014, http://www.cbn.com/cbnnews/us/2014/May/Divorce -Shocker-Most-Marriages-Do-Make-It/.

5 Richard P. Fitzgibbons, "The Risks of Cohabitation," accessed November 19, 2014, http://www.maritalhealing.com/conflicts/ risksofcohabitation.php.

6 Aaron Ben-Zeév, "In the Name of Love, A philosopher looks at our deepest emotion," *Psychology Today*, March 28, 2013, accessed November 14, 2014, https://docs.google.com/document/d/1J2j008v5D9uUR5r5QzIam7SQndEUbnoDqdxJUi7tK2I/editt emotion.

7 The Decline of Marriage and Rise of New Families, *Pew Research Social and Demographic Trends*, [November 18, 2010], accessed November 18, 2014, http://www.pewsocialtrends.org/2010/11/18/the-decline-of-marriage-and-rise-of-new-families/.

8 Emily Allen, "Falling divorce rates are 'a result of couples living together before marriage'", *Daily Mail.com News*, [September 23, 2011], accessed November 14, 2014, http://www.dailymail.co.uk/news/article-2040878/Falling-divorce-rates-result-couples-living-marriage.html.

9 Dan Hurley, Divorce Rate: It's Not As High As You Think, *New York Times, Health*, April 19, 2005, accessed February 15, 2014. http://www.nytimes.com/2005/04/19/health/19divo.html.

10 Paul Strand, "Divorce Shocker: Most Marriages Do Make It", *CBN News, US*, May 6, 2014, accessed February 15, 2015, http://www.cbn.com/cbnnews/us/2014/May/Divorce-Shocker-Most-Marriages-Do-Make-It/.

11 Randal Olson, October 10, 2014, comment on "What Makes for a Stable Marriage? October 10, 2014, accessed February 17, 2014. file:///home/chronos/u-f8cf0951dc1646f88ab1381f2d474aea1144102b/Downloads/ssrn-id2501480.pdf.

12 Paul Strand, "Divorce Shocker: Most Marriages Do Make It", *CBN News, US*, May 6, 2014, accessed February 15, 2015, http://www.cbn.com/cbnnews/us/2014/May/Divorce-Shocker-Most-Marriages-Do-Make-It/.

Chapter 2

1 John Paul II, "Homily: Solemn Mass for 17th World Youth Day," Vatican Website, July 28, 2002, no. 3, accessed February

17, 2015, http://www.vatican.va/holy_father/john_paul_ii/ homilies/2002/documents/hf_jp-ii_hom_20020728_xvii-wyd _en.html.

2 John Paul II, "Homily: Solemn Mass for 17th World Youth Day," Vatican Website, July 28, 2002, no. 5, accessed February 17, 2015, http://www.vatican.va/holy_father/john_paul_ii/ homilies/2002/documents/hf_jp-ii_hom_20020728_xvii-wyd _en.html.

3 Note: all items in bulleted list format throughout this book are from the Witness to Love Training Material unless stated otherwise. All resources used from the Witness to Love: Marriage Prep Renewal Ministry Training Material are under copyright by the authors. Any questions regarding the referencing of this material must be directed to the authors and must be referred to as "Witness to Love Training Material." All discussion questions, reflections and suggestions in bullet list format must receive written permission from the authors to be reproduced.

Chapter 3

1 Matthew 25:14-30

Chapter 4

1 John Paul II, "Letter to Families", Vatican Website, 1994, no. 23, accessed January 10, 2015, http://w2.vatican.va/ content/john-paul-ii/en/letters/1994/documents/hf_jp-ii_let _02021994_families.html.

2 Rebecca Wind, Premarital Sex is Nearly Universal Among Americans, and Has Been for Decades, *Guttmacher Institute*, December 19, 2006, accessed January 15, 2015, http://www .guttmacher.org/media/nr/2006/12/19/.

3 Scott Stanley, comment on Sliding vs. Deciding, slidingvs-deciding.blogspot. January 23, 2015, http://slidingvsdeciding.blogspot.com/

Chapter 5

1 Catholic Church. *Catechism of the Catholic Church.* 2nd ed. Vatican: Libreria Editrice
Vaticana, 2000. Print. In-text citation: (Catholic Church 1022)
2 1 John 4:20
3 Excerpts from the English translation of the *Roman Missal* © 2010, International Committee on English in the Liturgy Corporation. All rights reserved.

Chapter 6

1 Smith, Adam (1776). *Wealth of Nations: An Inquiry Into the Nature and Causes of The Wealth of Nations,* Mobi Classics", (London: W. Strahan and T. Cadell, MobileReference.com, 2010 - 1283 Seiten), accessed February 11, 2015, https://docs.google.com/document/d/1J2j008v5D9uUR5r5QzIam7SQndEUbnoDqdxJUi7tK2I/edit#heading=h.ilmvlvwf8h5v.

Chapter 7

1 Adelaide Mena, "Catholics Continue to Have Lowest Divorce Rates, Report Finds," Catholic News Agency, accessed March 17, 2015, http://www.catholicnewsagency.com/news/catholics-continue-to-have-lowest-divorce-rates-report-finds/
2 "No Fault Divorce," Wikepedia, The Free Encyclopedia, accessed February 5, 2015, http://en.wikipedia.org/wiki/No-fault_divorce#History

3 "The USLegal Dictionary," USLegal, US Legal, Inc., accessed January 5, 2015, http://definitions.uslegal.com/n/no-fault -divorce/.

4 "The Taxpayer Costs of Divorce and Unwed Childbearing: First Ever Estimates for the Nation and All Fifty States, Institute for American Values, accessed February 23, 2015, http:// americanvalues.org/catalog/pdfs/COFF.pdf.

5 Po Bronson and Ashley Merryman, "Will This Marriage Last," *Time*, June 30, 2006, accessed February 23, 2015, http://content .time.com/time/nation/article/0,8599,1209784,00.html.

6 Rachel Sheffield, "Hooking Up, Shacking Up, and Saying 'I Do' ", September 10th, 2014, T*he Witherspoon Institute, Public Discourse*, accessed January 20, 2015. http://www .thepublicdiscourse.com/2014/09/13765/.

7 Randal S. Olson, "What Makes for a Stable Marriage", October 10. 2014, *Randal S. Olson*, accessed January 23, 2015, http://www.randalolson.com/2014/10/10/what-makes-for-a -stable-marriage/.

8 Ibid.

9 Dr. David Currie, "Marital Prayer Part 1: What Happens When a Couple Prays Together", Doing Family Right, Maximizing Your Most Important Relationships, January 14, 2013, http://www.doingfamilyright.com/marital-prayer-part-1 -what-happens-when-a-couple-prays-together/

10 Randal S. Olson, "What Makes for a Stable Marriage", October 10. 2014, *Randal S. Olson*, accessed January 23, 2015, http://www.randalolson.com/2014/10/10/what-makes-for-a -stable-marriage/.

11 Ibid.

12 Ibid.

13 Ibid.

14 Ibid.

15 Mom.me, "The Effect of Divorced Parents on a Child's Future Relationships: Tips to minimize the negative effects of a break-up," accessed February 5, 2015, http://mom.me/parenting/6576-effect-divorced-parents-childs-future-relationships/

16 Po Bronson and Ashley Merryman, "Will This Marriage Last?," *Time*, June 30, 2006, accessed February 20, 2014, http://content.time.com/time/nation/article/0,8599,1209784,00.html.

17 Tim B. Heaton, "Factors Contributing to Increasing Marital Stability in the United States," *Journal of Family Issues* 23 (2002): 392–409; W. Bradford Wilcox, "The Evolution of Divorce," *National Affairs* 1 (2009): 81–94.

18 Ibid.

19 Emily Esfahani Smith, "Masters of Love: Science says lasting relationships come down to—you guessed it—kindness and generosity," *The Atlantic*, June 12, 2014, accessed February 23, 2015, http://m.theatlantic.com/health/archive/2014/06/happily-ever-after/372573/.

20 Po Bronson and Ashley Merryman, "Will This Marriage Last?," *Time*, June 30, 2006, accessed February 20, 2014, http://content.time.com/time/nation/article/0,8599,1209784,00.html.

21 Cassandra Hough, " Learning About Love: How Sex Ed Programs Undermine Happy Marriages," *The Witherspoon Institute, Public Discourse*, October 14 ,2014, accessed January 20, 2015, http://www.thepublicdiscourse.com/2014/10/13831/.

22 Gary Chapman, *The Five Love Languages, The Secret to Love That Lasts,* (Chicago: Northfield, 2010) Print

Chapter 8

1 Update about our frozen wedding cake. When I used this example our wedding cake top was safely frozen in our freezer.

The night after I wrote this chapter our freezer died and our cake unhappily melted. The moral may be that your marriage should work better than your freezer.

2 American Chesterton Society, "A Defense of Rash Vows," accessed November 30, 2014, http://www.chesterton.org/a -defence-of-rash-vows/

3 Ibid.

4 Galatians 2:20

5 Hebrews 4:12

6 Emily Esfahani Smith, "Masters of Love", *The Atlantic*, June 12, 2014. accessed February 16, 2015, http://m.theatlantic .com/health/archive/2014/06/happily-ever-after/372573/

7 Ibid.

8 Ibid.

9 Daniel Goleman, "Marriage: Research Reveals Ingredients of Happiness", *The New York Times, Science,* April 16, 1985. accessed February 15, 2015, http://www.nytimes.com/1985/ 04/16/science/marriage-research-reveals-ingredients-of -happiness.html?module=Search&mabReward=relbias: w&pagewanted=1

10 Emily Esfhani Smith, "Masters of Love", *The Atlantic,* June 12, 2014. accessed February 16, 2015, http://m.theatlantic .com/health/archive/2014/06/happily-ever-after/ 372573/

11 Ibid.

12 Ecclesiastes 4:10

Chapter 9

1 John Paul II, "Homily: Apostolic Pilgrimage To Bangladesh, Singapore, Fiji Islands, New Zealand, Australia And Seychelles," Vatican Website, November 30, 1986, no. 6. Accessed November 28, 2014, http://w2.vatican.va/content/john-paul

-ii/en/homilies/1986/documents/hf_jp-ii_hom_19861130
_perth-australia.html.
2 Ibid.

Chapter 11

1 Matthew 19:8
2 Matthew 9:24-26
3 Lewis, C.S. *A Grief Observed*. New York: Harper & Row, 1961. Print.
4 Please note: We are not talking about instances of abusive relationships here. The Catholic Church provides for licit separation of spouses. See CCC 2383 (The separation of spouses while maintaining the marriage bond can be legitimate in certain cases provided for by canon law.) and CIC 1151-1155, esp. 1153 (If either of the spouses causes grave mental or physical danger to the other spouse or to the offspring or otherwise renders common life too difficult, that spouse gives the other a legitimate cause for leaving, either by decree of the local ordinary or even on his or her own authority if there is danger in delay.
5 2 Corinthians 1:3-4

Chapter 12

1 Hebrews 12:1
2 This is from the Solemn Blessing from Rite of Marriage, option 1.
3 Genesis 2:18
4 Religion, The 8 Best Quotes from Pope Francis' Inspiring Address to Families, *Aleteia*, Seekers of the Truth, October 28, 2013, http://www.aleteia.org/en/religion/article/

the-8-best-quotes-from-pope-francis-address-to-families
-8704001

5 Francis, "Address to To The Board Of Directors And Personnel Of The Television Network TV 2000," Vatican Website, December 15, 2014, accessed March 18, 2015, http://w2.vatican.va/content/francesco/en/speeches/2014/december/documents/papa-francesco_20141215_tv2000.html

6 John 17:20-22

Bibliography

1 John 4:20

2 Corinthians 1:3-4

Allen, Emily. "Falling divorce rates are 'a result of couples living together before marriage.'" *Daily Mail.com News*, September 23, 2011. Accessed November 14, 2014. http://www.dailymail .co.uk/news/article-2040878/Falling-divorce-rates-result -couples-living-marriage.html.

American Chesterton Society. "A Defense of Rash Vows." Accessed November 30, 2014. http://www.chesterton.org/a -defence-of-rash-vows/

Ben-Zeev, Aaron. "In the Name of Love, A philosopher looks at our deepest emotion." *Psychology Today*, March 28, 2013. Accessed December 20, 2014. https://www.psychologytoday .com/blog/in-the-name-love.

Bronson, Po and Ashley Merryman. "Will This Marriage Last." *Time*, June 30, 2006. Accessed Febrary 23, 2015. http://content .time.com/time/nation/article/0,8599,1209784,00.html.

Catholic Church. *Catechism of the Catholic Church. 2nd ed.* Vatican: Libreria Editrice Vaticana, 2000. Print. In-text citation: (Catholic Church 1022)

Chapman, Gary, *The Five Love Languages, The Secret to Love That Lasts*, Chicago: Northfield, 2010. Print.

Ecclesiastes 4:10

Excerpts from the English translation of Rite of Marriage are copyright © 1969, ICEL. All rights reserved. Individuals who wish to reproduce text from Rite of Marriage for their own use (including reproduction in wedding programs) must follow the ICEL copyright permission procedures, which may be found at www.icelweb.org. - See more at: http://catholicweddinghelp .com/topics/text-nuptial-blessing.htm#sthash.xdsvmsYO .dpuf

Excerpts from the English translation of the Roman Missal are copyright © 2010, International Committee on English in the Liturgy, Inc.

Fitzgibbons, Richard P. "The Risks of Cohabitation." Accessed November 19, 2014. http://www.maritalhealing.com/conflicts/ risksofcohabitation.php.

Galatians 2:20

Genesis 2:18

Goleman, Daniel. "Marriage: Research Reveals Ingredients of Happiness." *The New York Times, Science,* April 16, 1985. Accessed February 15, 2015. http://www.nytimes.com/1985/ 04/16/science/marriage-research-reveals-ingredients-of -happiness.html?module=Search&mabReward=relbias: w&pagewanted=1

Heaton, Tim B. "Factors Contributing to Increasing Marital Stability in the United States," Journal of Family Issues 23 (2002): 392–409; W. Bradford Wilcox, "The Evolution of Divorce," National Affairs 1 (2009): 81–94.

Hebrews 12:1

Hebrews 4:12

Hough, Cassandra. "Learning About Love: How Sex Ed Programs Undermine Happy Marriages." *The Witherspoon Institute, Public Discourse* (October 14 ,2014). Accessed January 20, 2015. http://www.thepublicdiscourse.com/2014/10/13831/.

Hurley, Dan. "Divorce Rate: It's Not As High As You Think." *New York Times, Health,* April 19, 2005. Accessed February 15, 2014. http://www.nytimes.com/2005/04/19/health/19divo .html.

John Paul II, "Apostolic Pilgrimage to Bangladesh, Singapore, Fiji Islands, New Zealand, Australia and Sechelles, Homily of John Paul II"Libreria Editrice Vaticana, Perth (Australia), 30 November 1986. http://www.2.vatican.va/content/john-paul-ii/en/homilies/1986/documents/hf_jp-ii_hom_19861130_perth-australia.html Paragraph 6

John Paul II, Pope. "WYD 2002 - Solemn Mass: Homily - Toronto, Downsview Park." *Vatican.va*, 2015. Accessed February 17, 2015. http://www.vatican.va/holy_father/john_paul_ii/homilies/2002/documents/hf_jp-ii_hom_20020728_xvii-wyd_en.html.

John Paul II, Pope. "Letter to Families, New Advent, Letter to Families." 1994. Accessed January 10, 2015. http://www.newadvent.org/library/docs_jp02lf.htm

John Paul II, Pope. "Redemptor Hominis", Papal Encyclicals Online, Pope St. John Paul II 1978-2005". Accessed 2/10/2014. http://www.papalencyclicals.net/JP02/.

Lewis, C.S. *A Grief Observed*. New York: Harper & Row, 1961. Print.

Martin, Dean. Memories Are Made Of This Lyrics | MetroLyrics, Listen to Song. Accessed February 19, 2015. http://www.google.com/url?q=http%3A%2F%2Fwww.metrolyrics.com%2Fmemories-are-made-of-this-lyrics-dean-martin.html%23ixzz3HRDetOBM&sa=D&sntz=1&usg=AFQjCNE9U8Qf9PhD0AI0oM0T1TADbAOLcQ

Matthew 25:14-30

Matthew 9:24-26

Mom.me, "The Effect of Divorced Parents on a Child's Future Relationships: Tips to minimize the negative effects of a break-up." Accessed February 5, 2015. http://mom.me/parenting/6576-effect-divorced-parents-childs-future-relationships/.

"No Fault Divorce." *Wikipedia, The Free Encyclopedia*. Accessed February 5, 2015. http://en.wikipedia.org/wiki/No-fault_divorce#History.

Olson, Randal S. October 10, 2014, comment on "What Makes for a Stable Marriage?" October 10, 2014, accessed February 17, 2014, file:///home/chronos/u -f8cf0951dc1646f88ab1381f2d474aea1144102b/Downloads/ ssrn-id2501480.pdf.

Olson, Randal S. "What Makes for a Stable Marriage." October 10. 2014, accessed January 23, 2015, http://www.randalolson .com/2014/10/10/what-makes-for-a-stable-marriage/.

"Pew Research Center, Marriage at All Time Low in US." *Press TV*, Last modified September 24, 2014. Accessed November 19, 2014. http://www.presstv.com/detail/2014/09/24/379867/ study-marriage-at-alltime-low-in-us/.

Scott Stanley, comment on Sliding vs. Deciding, slidingvsdeciding. blogspot. January 23, 2015, http://slidingvsdeciding.blogspot .com/

Sheffield,Rachel. "Hooking Up, Shacking Up, and Saying 'I Do'". September 10th, 2014. *The Witherspoon Institute, Public Discourse.* Accessed January 20, 2015. http://www .thepublicdiscourse.com/2014/09/13765/.

Smith,Adam (1776).Wealth of Nations: An Inquiry Into the Nature and Causes of The Wealth of Nations,Mobi Classics",(London: W. Strahan and T.Cadell,MobileReference.com,2010 - 1283 Seiten), accessed February 11,2015,https://docs.google.com/document/ d/1J2j008v5D9uUR5r5QzIam7SQndEUbnoDqdxJUi7tK2I/ edit#heading=h.ilmvlvwf8h5v.

Smith, Emily Esfahani. "Masters of Love." *The Atlantic*, June 12, 2014. Accessed February 16, 2015. http://m.theatlantic.com/ health/archive/2014/06/happily-ever-after/372573/.

Strand, Paul. "Divorce Shocker: Most Marriages Do Make It." *CBN News US*, May 6, 2014. Accessed November 19, 2014. http://www.cbn.com/cbnnews/us/2014/May/Divorce -Shocker-Most-Marriages-Do-Make-It/.

Strand, Paul. "Divorce Shocker: Most Marriages Do Make It." *CBN News US*, May 6, 2014. Accessed November 19,

2014. http://www.cbn.com/cbnnews/us/2014/May/Divorce
-Shocker-Most-Marriages-Do-Make-It/.

"The Decline of Marriage and Rise of New Families", Pew Research
Social and Demographic Trends,[November 18, 2010], accessed
November 18, 2014. http://www.pewsocialtrends.org/2010/11/
18/the-decline-of-marriage-and-rise-of-new-families/.

"The Taxpayer Costs of Divorce and Unwed Childbearing:First
Ever Estimates for the Nation and All Fifty States, Institue
for American Values, accessed February 23, 2015, http://
americanvalues.org/catalog/pdfs/COFF.pdf.

"The USLegal Dictionary," USLegal, US Legal, Inc., accessed January 5, 2015, http://definitions.uslegal.com/n/no-fault-divorce/.

Wind, Rebecca. "Premarital Sex is Nearly Universal Among
Americans, and Has Been for Decades." *Guttmacher Institute*,
December 19, 2006. Acessed January 15, 2015. http://www
.guttmacher.org/media/nr/2006/12/19/.

Resources

For marriages that need some extra help:

Alexander, Greg and Julie. *Marriage 911: How God Saved Our Marriage (and Can Save Yours, Too!)*. Servant Books, 2011.

Cloud, Henry. Townsend, John, *Boundaries in Marriage*. Zondervan Books, 2002.

Chapman, Gary. *The 5 Love Languages: The Secret to Love that Lasts*. Northfield Publishing, 2010.

Guarendi, Ray, Dr. *Marriage: Small Steps, Big Rewards*. St. Anthony Messenger Press, 2011.

Guarendi, Ray, Dr. *Fighting Mad: Practical Solutions for Conquering Anger*. Servant Books, 2013.

Olson, David., Sigg, Amy Olson. and Larson, Peter. *The Couple Checkup*. Thomas Nelson, 2008.

Williams, Joe and Michelle. *Yes, Your Marriage Can Be Saved*. Tyndale House Publishers, Inc. 2007).

National Institute of Marriage in Partnership with Williams, Joe and Michelle. *Marriage 911 First Response Workbook*. National Institute of Marriage, 2007.

Kendrick, Stephen and Alex. *The Love Dare*. B&H Publishing Group, 2008.

Schuchts, Bob, Dr. *Be Healed: A Guide to Encountering the Powerful Love of Jesus in Your Life*. Ave Maria Press, 2014.

Brush-up on the Theology of Marriage

Coffin, Patrick. *Sex au Naturel: What It Is and Why It's Good for Your Marriage*. Emmaus Road Publishing, 2010.

Fisher, Simcha. *The Sinner's Guide to Natural Family Planning*. Our Sunday Visitor, 2014.

Healy, Mary. *Men and Women Are From Eden: A Study Guide to John Paul II's Theology of the Body*. Servant Books, 2005.

Pope John Paul II, *The Role of Christian Family in Modern World by Pope John Paul II*. Daughters of St. Paul, 1981.

West, Christopher. *The Good News About Sex & Marriage*. Servant Books, 2007.

West, Christopher. *Heaven's Song: Sexual Love as it was Meant to Be*. Ascension Press, 2008.

Sri, Edward P. *Men, Women and the Mystery of Love: Practical Insights from John Paul II's Love and Responsibility*. Servant Books, 2007.

Marriage Enrichment and great gifts for "Newlyweds"

Bennett, Art and Laraine. *The Temperament God Gave Your Spouse*. Sophia Institute Press, 2008.

Cavins, Jeff and Pinto, Matthew and Armstrong, Patti. *Amazing Grace for Married Couples: 12 Life-Changing Stories of Renewed Love*. Ascension Press, 2005.

Petitfils, Roy. *What I Wish Someone Had Told Me About the First Five Years of Marriage*. St. Anthony Messenger Press, 2010

Popcak, Gregory K., Phd. *Holy Sex!: A Catholic Guide to Toe-Curling, Mind-Blowing, Infallible Loving*. The Crossroad Publishing Company, 2008.

Popcak, Gregory K., Phd. *For Better Forever: A Catholic Guide to Lifelong Marriage.* Our Sunday Visitor, 1999

Popcak, Gregory K., Phd. *The Exceptional Seven Percent: The Nine Secrets of the Worlds Happiest Couples.* Citadel, 2002.

Popcak, Gregory K. and Lisa. *Just Married: The Catholic Guide to Surviving and Thriving in the First Five Years of Marriage.* Ave Maria Press, 2013.

Sheen, Fulton. *Three to Get Married* by Fulton Sheen. Scepter Pubs, 1996.

Von Hildebrand, Alice. *By Love Refined: Letters to a Young Bride.* Sophia Institute Press, 1998.

Books to Share with "The Unmarried"

Eden, Dawn. *The Thrill of the Chaste (Catholic Edition): Finding Fulfillment While Keeping Your Clothes On.* Ave Maria Press, 2015.

Evert, Jason. *If You Really Loved Me: 100 Questions on Dating, Relationships and Sexual Purity.* Catholic Answers, 2002.

Harris, Joshua. I Kissed Dating Goodbye. Multnomah Books, 1997.

Lewis, C.S. *The Four Loves.* Mariner Books, 1971.

Vanauken, Sheldon. *A Severe Mercy.* Harper One, 2009.

Suggested Web Resources:

MarriageSavers.org
GaryChapman.org
http://www.foryourmarriage.org/
www.MaritalHealing.com
TheAlexanderHouse.org
Retrouvaille.org
http://www.domesticchurchfamilies.com/

http://www.coupleprayer.com/
http://thecommunicationcure.com/
http://www.agapecatholicministries.com/the-catholic-
   communication-cure
http://www.exceptionalmarriages.com/
www.couplecheckup.com

Acknowledgements

As we finish writing this book during the "busy months" for marriage preparation, we realize how much we missed having couples over during the slower winter months. With that said, we are humbled by the countless couples who shared their hearts with us and allowed us to share our hearts with them. It is for them that we ultimately wrote this book and opened our home in order that we might be so intimately involved in the development of their vocations and relationships with Christ. We are additionally grateful for the mentor couples who have given so much of their time and love to these young engaged couples and who have committed to accompanying them over the years. Your deep friendship and openness with each other has touched and encouraged us. It has been a joy to work with you over the years, and we look forward to the years to come! For those whose stories are shared in this book and for those stories we did not have room to tell, we want you to know how much we love you and thank God for you and your dedication.

We must also thank our pastor and friend, Fr. Michael Delcambre. Without Fr. Michael's guidance, openness to the Holy Spirit, and creative support, *Witness to Love* and this book never would not exist. Father, we thank you for your friendship, your trust, and your love for marriage and family, for Christ, and for His Church. We thank you for allowing us to be a part of your ministry and for being the Spiritual Advisor to *Witness to Love.* Your priesthood and life are a great gift to us all, and we love you dearly!

To all those who have covered us with prayers and support while we wrote this book, we offer our gratitude, especially to: Lydia, Sr. Agnes Mary Quartararo, O.P, Fr. Matt Williams, Anne-Christian, and Blair and Derek. Your prayers helped us to persevere!

To those who have encouraged *Witness to Love* and guided us in developing this ministry, we thank you for your wisdom and support: Archbishop Gregory Aymond, Bishop Michael Jarrell, Fr. Andrew Merrick, Mr. Rickard Newman and Mr. David Dawson.

To those couples who have mentored us or been an inspiration to us over the years, we treasure your friendship and offer you our prayers and love: Eleanor and Joe, Dr. Greg & Miss Erin, Nancy & Kelly, David & Kate, Missy & Kyle, Geoff & Lauren, Adam & Marianne, Sandra & Eric, and John & Moya.

To our spiritual directors and those who have given us counsel over the years, especially thank: Bishop Sam Jacobs, Fr. Tom Dilorenzo, Fr. Michael Champagne, Fr. Thomas Vander Woude, Fr. Chris Pollard, Dr. Frank Moncher and Dr. Bob Schuchts. Thank you for your love and wisdom.

We thank Jill who is a gift to us and to our family. Everyone wonders how we found the time to write this book with work and three little children. Our answer is always, "Jill." No one can write a book without a "Jill." We thank you

Jill for all the hours that you taught, distracted, loved, and enjoyed our children while we were working on this project. You brought order and peace to a time that could have been quite chaotic otherwise.

We also want to thank Jay and Michelle Wonacott for their expertise and guidance with the writing of this book. Working with you both took this to a whole new level of accessibility, and we are sure the readers would thank you if they knew how much easier this book is to read because of you! Anne Angelle, we want to thank you for the many hours you put into proofreading the original manuscript for us. We are so grateful for your encouragement, prayers, excitement, and tireless efforts when the work was tedious. Fr. Eric Cadin, thank you for coming to the rescue at the last minute and proof- reading the entire final manuscript into the wee hours of the morning before we turned it in. We are so blessed by your dedication and your friendship!

We want to thank Conor, Rick, Christian, Paul, Mara, Caroline, and all the staff at St. Benedict Press for believing in this book and asking us to write it. Thank you to each of you for sharing your wisdom and expertise with us.

We must of course thank our parents for the gift of our lives and for all they taught us! Life continues to teach us that we should never take for granted the gift of family. With that said, we include a special prayer of thanksgiving for our children, Zélie, André, and Mélodie Rose. They put up with a lot during this process and are very intimately involved in *Witness to Love*! Having a five-, three- and one-year-old around during opportunities of ministry is always exciting! They have always possessed a unique interest in our work and always made themselves quite comfortable on our laps during mentoring sessions and periods of work on our laptops! If there are any typos in this book, we give all the credit to our children's creativity and personal commitment to this endeavor!

Finally we thank our Lord for the gift of Marriage and for the grace that this sacrament daily offers to us. We are grateful for the intercession of all the holy marriages that have gone before us and in particular, to our patrons, Blessed Louis and Zélie Martin. The heroic way that they welcomed children into the world and remained faithful to their union is a consistent model of generosity to God and to one's spouse. We also thank and praise God, our Father in Heaven for the gift of Jesus Christ that was born into the beautiful marriage of Mary and Joseph of Nazareth. May the mysterious gift of the Incarnate Word born in Bethlehem, held in the secure arms of matrimony, remain a constant witness of God's enduring love for each and every one of us!

About the Authors

RYAN and Mary-Rose Verret are the Founders of *Witness to Love: Marriage Preparation Renewal Ministry*, a movement dedicated to renewing the way engaged couples perceive and receive marriage preparation. *Witness to Love* provides training, resources, and ongoing support for clergy and those engaged in marriage preparation. Particularly, *Witness to Love* is a resource for those who recognize the essential and urgent need to integrate engaged couples fully into the life of their church community. Ongoing involvement in one's church is proven to be one of the most important components of supporting couples in a life-long commitment to the covenant of matrimony.

Ryan and Mary-Rose are also certified Prepare-Enrich (PMI) instructors and give certification workshops around the United States. Together they have appeared on EWTN's *Life on the Rock*, and worked one-on-one with countless engaged couples, mentor couples, clergy and marriage preparation personnel. Mary-Rose has worked in diocesan and church level marriage ministry since 2005, and is a certified SymptoPro Fertility Awareness (NFP) instructor and trainer and has taught hundreds of couples in person and online. She has taught NFP to couples from India, Brazil,

Russia, Europe, Canada, and the United States. Mary-Rose enjoys working with couples who have experienced infertility, and gives lectures on the use of Fertility Awareness Methods (FEMs) to identify and treat cycle-related issues and infertility. Ryan completed graduate studies in Theology, Clinical Psychology, and Medical Ethics and worked for several years in the field of healthcare administration. Since 2010, Ryan has worked primarily in the development of legislative and educational efforts that develop the Culture of Life both in Louisiana and throughout the United States and Canada.

Together Ryan and Mary-Rose speak on issues regarding fertility, IVF, marriage, NFP, and euthanasia. They are frequent guests on EWTN's *Catholic Radio for Acadiana* and they reside in the heart of Cajun Country with their three children. Their passion is teaching couples to share their marriage with others!